Northwest Vista Coll. ✍ **Y0-CQS-303**
Learning Resource Center
3535 North Ellison Drive
San Antonio, Texas 78251

# Building Blocks of Light

## Teaching Students with Learning Disabilities How to Improve Their Minds

### Building Blocks of Light
### A guide for Counselors

### and

### Elementary School Educators

By

## Margaret Laurie

This book is a work of non-fiction. Names and places have been changed to protect the privacy of all individuals. The events and situations are true.

ISBN: 1-4140-0432-X (e-book)
ISBN: 1-4140-0433-8 (Paperback)
ISBN: 1-4184-7251-4 (Dust Jacket)
Library of Congress Control Number: 2003097125

This book is printed on acid free paper.

Printed in the United States of America
Bloomington, IN

1stBooks - rev. 05/13/04

# Preface

Helping others to learn is easy—when you know how the human brain works. I discovered the secret when I found Altered States of Awareness[1] a collection of articles by fourteen Engineers, Scientists and other experts which had been previously published by Scientific American.

Simply put, authors of the articles explain that the human brain has four basic vibrational patterns. Those which allow us to cope with the world about us start with 13 vibrations per second and are called Beta Rhythms.

But when the brain slows to between 12 and 7 vibrations per second—the Alpha Level - learning, problem solving, and all other mental exercises become remarkably easy.

Slowed further to the Theta Level—between 6 and 4 vibes per second—the brain falls asleep. Deep sleep occurs when brain activity drops to the Delta Level—five vibes a second.

---

[1] Timothy J. Tyler et al, Altered States of Awareness. San Francisco, California:W. H. Freeman and Company, 1972.

The Alpha Level is where we think clearly, learn, solve our problems, and heal our bodies. My book Centering Your Guide to Inner Growth, which was prompted by the brain level discoveries, has helped adults achieve their goals since its first publication in 1978. Building Blocks of Lights will now do the same for children. This work resulted from a year of teaching an ADD youngster how to slow her brain activity in order to reduce her physical problems and learn easily. Two brief chapters of Lynn's experiences are followed by Building Block exercises for educationally challenged children.

Good students know how to concentrate: that is, ignore their surroundings enough to slow their brains to the Alpha level. Poor students, on the other hand, must be taught how to turn off the world of the five senses and become comfortable in Alpha.

Although the 12-7 vibrations per second area became synonymous with Extra Sensory Perception (ESP) during the Twentieth Century, we now know there is nothing weird or occult about it. It is a normal brain level that can turn academically challenged students into competent learners.

Many counselors and teachers at the Elementary Level already use Guided Imagery to calm their classes. But Building Blocks of Light goes further—its information will enable you to help children "settle down and learn." It works wonders in a hyper-child emergency, but is equally great and more cost-effective for small group sessions. Some of the Blocks, especially A to D, are suitable for a full class, but those which require student interaction will be more effective with at least four but no more than six participants. Use the techniques at school and encourage parents to become acquainted with the procedures and reinforce them at home.

Now, let me introduce you to Lynn, an ADD child whose success led to Building Blocks of Light.

# Table of Contents

# Chapter 1

## Session 1, May 5, 1996

As my friend Jeanne and her granddaughter, Lynette Herson, started up my driveway, I wondered whether I was doing the right thing. I am not a psychiatrist, psychologist or physician, but an English Professor who wrote and taught an accredited course in meditation at my College for over a dozen years. My students were teenagers and adults. What could I do for a child whom Jeanne had said was eight years old but looked far younger? Lynn entered my house and introduced herself in proper grown-up fashion. I stooped to greet and put her at ease. Her brown hair was lustrous but her tiny face lacked expression and her eyes looked dull. While I hung up her jacket, she inched past me to study the decor of my living room. Grownups often do the same. Brick red walls are not to everyone's taste. But the color scheme livens up visitors.

It certainly worked for Lynn. Two steps inside the living area she turned into a whirling dervish. She fingered the plant on the coffee table and picked up my Garden of Eden pillow to tug at the two-inch, three-dimensional figures of Adam, Eve, and accompanying angels. Then, in a flash, she raced past her grandmother and slipped behind a chair to pick trinkets from my bookshelves. Nothing escaped her scrutiny or held her attention for long. On examining and asking about a bird statue, she didn't wait to hear that the bird was the pagan god Horus, but exchanged it for an Egyptian sarcophagus. Within two minutes she had fondled and replaced every movable object she could reach on the shelves, and sped to other bookshelves.

On agreeing to see Lynn, I had asked Jeanne to let the child do as she liked. Before I could help her in any way, I had to see her in action.

Next, she darted into the dining room, paused to look around and raced into the kitchen.

When Jeanne called her back, Lynn returned, passed us and bounded up the stairs to investigate the upper floor. Jeanne leaped up, but I urged her to wait. Curiosity was a sign of intelligence, I said, as Lynn pounded through the rooms above us and came hurtling down the stairwell.

"Look what I found," she said, holding out toys which had been on a shelf behind a screen in the master bedroom.

Jeanne opened her mouth to protest, but I assured her I kept the toys for visitors. "Lynn can play with them all she likes. She just can't take them out of the house."

"Why not?" asked Lynn, looking me up and down as if to say I was too old to own a pyramid pillow, a stuffed camel, and the witch from the Broom Hilda comic strips.

"Why? Because they were gifts, and I never give those away," I said. "You see that camel? My grandson was two years old when he found the "drawmadery" and claimed it for his own. He wanted it. Oh, how he wanted it. So—I had to find another one. It took me two weeks, but Mark finally got his own "drawmadery" and left mine to play with when he visited."

Forgetting her interest in the camel, Lynn poked at the tan pyramid pillow, pulled out the inserted cloth "block" and squealed with delight at finding a blue mummy inside.

3

The pyramid held her interest about twenty seconds longer. Broom Hilda lasted ten seconds. Then she scooted to the first bookshelf, picked off the stone sarcophagus and put it on the floor between two other objects relating to Egypt, the stuffed camel and pyramid pillow.

I chuckled at this evidence of intelligence and she whipped her head around and gave me a grin. Better yet, the eyes which had looked so flat, expressionless and dark came alive for a second. I was surprised to see they were light blue. Having gained her attention, I told her we were going to play a game. Seating myself on the carpet, I asked Lynn to put her gum on a plate, sit down someplace and close her eyes.

The someplace turned out to be my lap. My surprise at having an eight-year-old react in a manner befitting a much younger child soon gave way to discomfort. Even "at rest," Lynn was a whirlwind. Her arms flailed and her hands struck my chest and head. Her legs twitched and jumped, causing the rough edges of her shoes to dig into my leg bones. Every part of her was on the move and I could not escape. Nor did I want to. If this was the price of establishing a firm relationship, I would pay it gladly. My bruises or pains would pass. Hers would not. Lynn needed help. Desperately.

Ignoring the assault on my midriff and legs, I closed my eyes and said in a soft whisper, "Close your eyes, Lynn, and pretend you're inside your chest. Though it's dark now, there's a Light in there. The Light's small at first. Just a tiny pinprick, for most of us. But it's there. Look around and find it. Shhh, now. Search. And let me know when you see it," I said in a low, relaxed voice.

Within a minute Lynn found the Light. As she did, her limbs quieted and she curled up into the fetal position. I praised her for being so quick, and she responded by churning her arms and legs again. She needed approval. People with disabilities rarely get the positive feedback that builds healthy self-respect. Lynn was desperate for kind words. Having got them, the tension in her extremities lessened and she resumed the fetal position.

Continuing softly, I said, "This Light you've found in yourself, Lynn, is the most important thing on earth. It's the Light of life. Actually, it's the Light of Holy Spirit and every one of us has it."

Still curled up in my lap like an unborn child, she asked, "Why didn't I find it before?"

"You didn't look. Few people do. At least until they're told it exists. Now—oh, close your eyes again. You'll need to keep them closed, too, to find the Light that shines down on you from above. Though we're inside the house at the moment, the Light is brilliant as sunlight. Think about that. Sunlight pours down on everyone, whether the person is good or bad. That's because every human being is special to the power of the universe that we call Spirit or God."

Lynn jumped as the small clock on my fireplace mantel chimed the hour. "What's that?" she cried in alarm, straightening her body and setting her legs and elbows into motion again.

"Just the clock. It's loud, isn't it? So
loud I hear it in my bedroom and know what
time it is during the night."

"It ticks loud, too," she said.

"Yes it does," I murmured. "That's because my house is so quiet."

Lynn twisted on my lap and peered up at
my face. "Why don't you turn on the TV? Or
the stereo?"

"They make too much noise, Lynn. Noise
keeps us from using the Light. We'll talk
about that later. Right now, we must close our
eyes again, find the Light within, and begin
to feel it filling our bodies."

"Oh. How we gonna do that?"

"First we have to recognize that Light
shines down on us from above. Then we take a
deep breath. As we breathe in, we breathe in
the Light from above and bring it down through
the top of our heads to our chests. There it
will join the Light within us. As we breathe
out, we breathe out any aches, pains, worries,
tensions or fears that might use up space in
our chests."

"Close your eyes and we'll start. Good
girl. Breathe in the Light and watch it come

down into your chest. Wonderful. Breathe out anything that bothers you. Breathe in Light again. Breathe out bad feelings. Oh, you did that perfectly. See how light your chest feels? It almost weightless, isn't it? Now look inside it. What was once dark is now shining with Light."

Lynn's body straightened and her limbs were stilled as she asked what we were going to do with the Light.

"Fill the rest of our bodies, for starters. You ready? Good. Inhale. That means breathe in. Exhale means breathe out. Exhale now, and empty your head of everything that rattles around in there."

"Inhale and let the Light fill your head. Exhale and empty your shoulders, arms and hands of any tightness. Inhale and let the Light fill your shoulders, arms and hands."

"Now your whole upper body is filled with Light, and feels as if it could float off into space. Doesn't that feel good?"

Lynn gave me a faint yes, but her body told me more. Her arms and hands were quiet, and we had only to bring the Light to her lower torso, legs and feet to control their restlessness. In three additional breaths, Lynn was filled from top to toe with Light and lying straight and peaceful on my lap.

The calm lasted fifty seconds. As I watched, Lynn turned her head and gave me a wide-eyed look. "I want to open my eyes," she said.

"You already did," I replied with a laugh. "What do you want to do now?"

As though I had given a signal, her arms and legs resumed their frantic dance. "Play with the toys," she said, jumping off my lap and using the soft Broom Hilda doll to hammer the camel, the pyramid, and the stone sarcophagus.

Two minutes later she lost interest in the toys, reseated herself on my lap and found the Light immediately. When I asked what inner part of her she wanted to investigate, she chose her left ear. Expecting she might need healing, I told her to follow the Light from her chest up through her throat to her nose and the tube that led to her left ear.

"You know, Lynn, Spiritual Light can heal us," I said.

Her limbs, which had been quiet for a bit, started to twitch and jump. "I don't hurt anyplace," she whispered.

"That's great, honey," I whispered back. "But sometime you might. So let's practice using the Light to heal. Let's bring more Light from above down into every part of your left ear. Ready? Take a deep breath. Breathe in the Light that enters the top of your head and send it to your ear. Great. Now, breathe out anything left over from a past ailment or injury. Do it three times at least. If you ever have an ache or pain in any part of your body, bring in the Light and let it do its healing. Then you may need seven or more full breaths to do the job. But three's enough for practice."

I added, "The Light helps in other ways. We need to be calm and collected. So, when we're feeling excited or worried, we should stop, close our eyes a moment, and find the Light within us. You think you can do it?"

When she murmured a soft yes, I tapped her shoulder in approval. "Wonderful. And will you practice twice a day—each night before you fall asleep, and every morning when

10

you awake? So you'll know what to do when you get excited?"

To emphasize the instruction, I gave her a three inch Ivory soap angel. Clutching this first present, she promised to practice finding the Light. Her grandmother said she would tell Lynn's mother to remind her, and asked when would be a good time to bring Lynn again.

The child wanted to come the next day, May 6, but Gramma and I thought it best to leave time between visits, and settled on May 11. When Lynn threw on her jacket and left the house to look around the yard, I told Jeanne that her granddaughter was a bright child—too bright to be in a Special Education class—but we would have to solve her physical problems to enable her to attend graded classrooms.

Lynn left our session far calmer than she had been at the start, but I wondered how long the effect of the child-meditation would last.

An hour later Lynn's mother, Marilyn, called to report some encouraging progress. On arriving home with her grandmother, Lynn sat calmly on her mother's lap and told of finding "the Light inside her." When her younger sister laughed, Lynn said it wasn't funny. For a while the eight-year-old remained seated and quietly talked with her Mom and Gramma. Then she left to go down to the rec room and play by herself.

Her mother was amazed. This was the first time Lynette had ever wanted to be alone, or even to leave the room when grownups were chatting. She always required her sister Ruth or someone else to entertain her. And she remained in the rec room so long that Ruth went down to join her.

Jeanne called that evening to say that when Lynn was four months old, her Mom put her in a reputable daycare facility and returned to her job. Within a few weeks Lynn had an infection in one ear and started to lose weight. Jeanne, who lives a distance away, went to her daughter's house to nurse the infant back to health, but Lynn kept having relapses until Marilyn quit her job and stayed home with her baby.

Lynn improved a bit, though she still ate poorly and her physical development lagged behind that of her peers. In kindergarten, she was the smallest and frailest of the group. When Marilyn inquired about Lynn's progress, she was told all children were inconsistent at that age.

At age seven and in the first grade, Lynn's problems increased. While her class-mates were completing worksheets on their own, Lynn needed someone to explain every step. Further, she ran her letters and words to-gether so no one could understand what she was writing. Though her parents hired a reading tutor, her grades grew steadily worse.

Three months before Lynn finished First Grade, the family moved. Concerned about Lynn's development, her mother and father asked the elementary educators in their new area to test her.

Marilyn described this as a hectic time. School authorities reported Lynn's IQ almost negligible. Her evaluators—teachers of Read-ing, Mathematics, Language and Speech, along with an Occupational Therapist and a Psycholo-gist—found the most consistent thing about Lynn was her inconsistency. On the IQ test, for example, she answered questions that stumped her peers, but often could not respond to what they found easy.

The entire panel of experts rated Lynn below average for her age, classified her as Learning Disabled, and recommended that the eight-year-old be placed in a Second Grade Special Education class for the next year. There Lynn and eleven other students would have the attention of one teacher and an aide, and receive regular help from Speech and Occupational Therapists.

Because Lynn loved everyone, she usually became a teacher's pet and thus got the individual attention she needed. But her first grade teacher, who had taught twenty years and knew children, described Lynn as an enigma. She said the child was sometimes attentive in class. Other times she just stared out the window. During her attentive periods she always had her hand up, but the answers she gave rarely fit the questions. In reading she could not identify the letter T. If it were pointed out to her, she lost it on the turn of a page.

Even so, her first grade teacher believed Lynn would catch up when she became "developmentally ready."

The Hersons fretted over Lynn's difficulties, especially her habit of curling into the fetal position when her mother held her. Fred told of taking Lynn to pediatricians, psychiatrists, neurologists and neuro-psychologists, whose only suggestions for treatment were Ritalin or a similar medication.

The Hersons did not want to expose their child to drugs and searched for some other cure. None seemed to appear, and then they learned that her sister, who was two years younger than Lynn, had faulty vision and might lose the sight of an eye. Further, Marilyn was pregnant with a third child.

Family turmoil increased when Lynn entered Second Grade.

Her special education teacher, struggling with two misbehaving students, could not give her the help she needed. When she fell hopelessly behind, Marilyn and Fred hired another Special Education teacher to test Lynn's abilities and to tutor her.

Using the Brigance Test of basic learning skills, the tutor found that in her Second Grade, seventh month of schooling, Lynn scored in one category: at First Grade, fourth month level in Math.

From what Lynn's mother and grandmother had said, Lynn had much catching up to do. I hoped meditation would calm her down so she could concentrate and learn like other children. In our first session she had immediately found and accepted the Light. Within a couple hours, she did two things for the first time: sat quietly on her mother's lap, and went off to play by herself. Such changes were encouraging, but we would have to wait and see whether these behavioral changes were permanent.

# Chapter 2

At our second meeting, Lynn chose to take an imaginary journey to Lake Chautauqua. Her description of the trip proved faster than light. Within one minute she arrived at the Lake, sailed across it, bought and devoured a hotdog, returned home and asked if she could open her eyes. Talk about short attention spans!

Lynn's had to be lengthened, so I requested a replay—in slow motion. She cooperated well and having found flash-impressions inacceptable, started to flesh out her story. The trip downstate, the ride on the boat across the Lake, eating the hotdog and similar details had to be drawn out of her at first. Once she understood that visualization requires more than the "been there, done that" of her initial recital, she took pleasure in spinning out her yarn.

The session lasted an hour, and concluded with a relaxed and calm eight-year old who was looking forward to her next adventure in the Light.

Two days later Jeanne told me that her daughter was going to Florida for a week, leaving Lynn and her two sisters with a baby-sitter. The news upset Lynn, and she seemed ready to jump out of her skin when Jeanne brought her for our May 17 meeting. When urged to find the Light, Lynn did so immediately, and built up enough to fly herself and her whole family down to Lake Chautauqua. But first she had to describe what every person was wearing, the purchase of hotdogs aboard the boat and what happened when her baby sister smeared catsup over her face and clothing. Her observations during that hour were heartening, for in using her imagination, she lengthened her attention span. Previously she had packed a day's events into a wad which she tossed aside. ADD people need to slow their brain waves. Lynn did it by slowing her breathing and "finding the Light." That done, she could relate her thoughts step by step.

The greatest benefit of our first three sessions was Lynn's ability to use the Light to calm herself. She succeeded so well that she astounded her entire family by being a "perfect angel" at home and school during her

Mother's weeklong visit to Florida. I rewarded her "behavioral breakthrough" with a second soap angel.

As she clutched it at the start of meditation 4, she said her Light was bigger than it used to be and filled all of her. And she wanted to use it to go over a rainbow. Which we did, with her describing the colors of the span, what lay below it, and the elf who had to surrender his imaginary gold to her.

At session 5, Jeanne brought Lynn's mother Marilyn to learn what we were doing, so she could help Lynn with "meditation home-work." Our student wanted to go over the rain-bow again. We used our Light to fly to Niagara Falls in Canada, where the rainbow started, but at the far end we could not set foot on Goat Island in the U. S. The elf of the previ-ous meditation, it seemed, had not replaced the imaginary gold. With nothing to anchor its end, the rainbow faded off into the air and we had to retrace our steps to Canada. Lynn then had to describe her father's car and the ride home to her house in New York State. Her at-tention span had expanded mightily, and when she could not remember the number of doors on the car or the color of her house, she learned to use the Light to see necessary details.

At our June 6, 1996 meeting, Lynn helped her sister Ruth find the Light and use it to heal her bad eye. We then rewarded ourselves with an imaginary visit to Disney World, where Lynn astounded us all by inventing a family which occupied the seats we had vacated on the Disney train. Her description of the parents and their two children made we want to leap into the air and click my heels.

At the next meeting Lynn and I taught her father Fred how to meditate. They became so relaxed that they slept for nine minutes. For her good work, Lynn earned a small clay pot filled with chocolates wrapped as coins—a tangible pot of gold to replace the imaginary one from rainbow's end.

At our eighth meditation, 6/21/96, Lynn quietly stretched out on the floor, with only her head in my lap. Further evidence of a "touchy-feely" behavior modification came when her Second Grade teachers no longer had to impose a limit of two-hugs-a-day.

At our ninth session, when Lynn spoke of her newly found Guardian Angel, I asked her to stand beside Rose and describe her own hair and clothing. Following our initial "detachment" exercise, Lynn visualized herself answering teacher's questions correctly and getting high grades in all her subjects.

Visualizing requires keen viewing, so on July 13 of '96 I asked Lynn to describe the people she met during summer art classes. These were conducted at our well-known attraction, Artpark, which offers children's programs as well as celebrity performances for adults. At first, Lynn remembered nothing. When she closed her eyes and recreated the scene, she described two of her instructors. The effort tired her, however, and she fell asleep.

During her nap, I gave her a lesson in math to help her count without using her fingers. I asked her to visualize on her mental screen numbers from 10+1 to 10+19. That done, she was to erase "0" and "+" and move the right hand number beside 1, for 11, 12, and so forth. We repeated the visualization for double digit 20 through 90 sequences. When she awoke, I tested her and, without using her fingers, she answered quickly and correctly.

Then she visualized herself facing a classroom blackboard and shouting out the answers to such numbers as 22 and 35

$$\underline{+8} \qquad \underline{+7}.$$

Her totals were correct, but Lynn had a Math Disability, so we had to wait until school resumed to find out if the lesson took.

At our next meeting, Lynn visualized herself preparing for school. We took it step by step, with her handling everything without assistance, from awaking to performing admirably in class. Following meditation, she picked coins of every denomination from a plate, using several combinations to make a dollar.

By our twelfth meeting, in August, Lynn was ready to conduct the meditation. She took us to the heavens where, she said, purple angels and pink ones were crossing a purple bridge. Her choice of purple was impressive, for it is a spiritual shade.

For the thirteenth session, an imaginary visit to Howe Caverns, I emphasized the similarity between earth processes and meditation. Like the river, we plunge into darkness and scour out a cavern for the Light. What we learn in the depths we bring back to the surface, be it earth or daily life. Visualizing success in the classroom followed the fictional trip.

Since Lynn would return to school after our next meeting, we devoted our August 30, 1996 hour to "foreseeing" successful classroom experiences.

Our next session came after school started. Lynn's two and a half days in the classroom had turned her "hyper." When I asked her to find the Light, she kept saying "Da da" and otherwise acting like an infant. She also sat on my lap (a practice discarded in June) and kicked her legs. We discussed using the Light to be calm, and she quieted down and went to sleep for fifteen minutes. By the time she left, she was in control of herself again.

On our sixteenth meeting, in mid-September, Lynn's grandmother reported a major Behavioral adjustment. Jeanne said that in her Second Grade year, Lynn resisted doing homework and required constant prodding and help. Her mother or another adult had to sit her down, position her papers and books, and guide her pencil for even simple assignments. Now, at the start of Third Grade, Lynn arrived home from school, seated herself at the kitchen table and completed every bit of homework before handing it to her mother.

As a reward, I presented her with a tiny solar calculator so she could check her Math answers. She showed more interest in the directions, but the print of the tiny folder was so small I brought out a magnifying glass. She read the directions aloud, needing help with just a few words like "electrical energy," then used the magnifying glass to read us a newspaper article that accompanied my grandson's picture.

Lynn had started to master her ADD symptoms, for her music teacher said she showed tremendous improvement in concentration when she played a difficult Mozart piece.

For these breakthroughs I promised her I would go to her school and teach her classmates how "to find the Light."

At our next meeting Lynn, her sister Ruth, her mother and I went to Australia on our imaginary journey that interposed fact and fiction.

Shortly after Lynn celebrated her ninth birthday in October, we learned the results of her second Brigance Diagnostic Inventory of Basic Skills test. The following compares the scores of the seventh month of Second Grade (2.7) with those earned after twenty one-hour meditations but ONLY three months of school— (3.2).

|              | Grade | Test Score | Grade | Test Score |
|--------------|-------|------------|-------|------------|
| Word Recog.  | (2.7) | 2.0        | (3.2) | 2.7        |
| Reading      | (2.7) | 1.0        | (3.2) | 2.0        |
| Math         | (2.7) | 2.2        | (3.2) | 3.5        |

Lynn's improvement was dramatic, but our goal was to bring her up to grade level.

Halloween 1996 was coming and we used the imaginary journey of Session Twenty for trick-or-treating practice. Lynn, who was making her own costume, described how she was painting and gluing plastic balls to strips of paper to turn herself into an old-fashioned Candy Strip.

As she spoke she started to bounce on my couch. When I reminded her of my house rule, no jumping on furniture, she told me she had been given a good role in Nutcracker Suite. Now I knew why she had been restless and fidgety three sessions in a row. She was dealing with a new school year, music lessons, Tricks and Treating excitement, and tryouts for a ballet. Like many ADD individuals, Lynn thrives on stimulation. But she was bringing her over-excitability under control through meditation.

Lynn's Halloween adventure proved a triumph. When she arrived at our twenty-first meeting, she told of winning First Prize for her own-made costume. Her prize was special coins: real money, not the foil covered chocolate ones of her pots of gold.

After congratulating her for her improved scores AND her great prize, we resumed visualizing success in school.

Proof of that arrived during Session 22, when Lynn brought a note from a speech teacher and asked me to read it. It said: "Dear Mrs. Herson. Today we worked on organizing our thoughts to describe pictures for a game we were playing. Lynn did a wonderful job of expressing herself. She also was focused for the entire session."

Our meditation had to do with pumpkins that found their own Light. In the succeeding week, Session 23, we practiced building and projecting Light. All went well until November 20, 1996, when Lynn's mother called for help. That morning Lynn had danced in the opening performance of The Nutcracker Suite, and had become too "hyper" to perform that afternoon. I agreed to meet Lynn immediately.

The child was almost completely out of control when she arrived at my house. Knowing she would be unable to find the Light then, I told her to take a deep breath and hold it while she said the word "CALMMM." Then she was to breathe out and repeat "CALMMM." She interrupted with aimless talk but after twenty breaths, she began to settle down. Fifteen minutes later she and her mother fell asleep. I filled the five minutes of their nap with positive suggestions and when they awoke Lynn said she had planned to nap when she got home. Now she felt so good she would play games with her sisters.

I attended Nutcracker Suite that afternoon and her newfound self-control allowed her to turn in a beautiful performance.

Lynn brought a Jingle Bells mood to Session 25 (12/2/96) and insisted on singing the entire song. Again, meditation calmed her and she worked on visualizing success in a Fourth Grade Classroom.

In mid-December, Jeanne and Lynn came loaded with Christmas presents, and insisted on hanging their gifts. One was a gorgeous wreathe decorated with an exquisite paper angel, and the other a magnificent gold angel from France. After we hung them above my fireplace, I told Lynn that it was time to get back to work. Straight-faced and solemn eyed, she said loudly, **"AND GET IT OVER WITH."**

Though children anticipating a ton of toys are not inclined to be serious, Lynn practiced foreseeing herself earning top grades in school.

Three days after Christmas we held our 27$^{th}$ session, with Lynn reporting on her presents from Santa, including those he delivered from me. But she longed to continue the holiday mood and used our imaginary journey to be a Christmas tree.

While fir trees fit the season, our initial session in the New Year featured her becoming an oak that stands sturdy and firm in the highest winds.

Lynn began our 29th meeting with a stomach ache and a loud claim that she had NEVER seen the Light. After we discussed my doubts about seeing it when I started to teach myself meditation, we identified and solved Lynn's real problem: anger at her parents going out to dinner every Friday night.

On her next visit, Lynn brought two of her artworks, one of which featured orange sunspots surrounded by raindrops. For our imaginary trip during Session 30, she chose to visit her painted raindrops. She enjoyed it so much that we repeated it for Sessions 31 and 32.

At Sessions 33 she asked for another raindrop experience—as a reward for getting good marks on her report card. I suggested going to the desert, but when she insisted on Australia, we compromised on the Australian desert.

I assumed that Lynn's excitability at our 34th meeting was due to having three houseguests, but her mother reported otherwise. After Lynn's great report card, her teacher introduced advanced Math and Spelling lessons. Unable to keep up, Marilyn explained, Lynn was reverting to her former habits. Thus, the bulk of our session was a discussion of Plateaus on the Learning Curve—which you will find in detail in your Building Block sections.

On March 10, 1997, I taught an Inner City Option One class how to "find the Light." Some of the Kindergarten through Second Grade students resisted the initial meditation, but the second time around all thirteen closed their eyes tightly and walked over the rainbow to the Buffalo zoo, where they claimed the Leprechaun's gold. As a reward, each received a bag of chocolates wrapped like gold coins.

During our 34$^{th}$ get-together, Lynn and I explored the meanings of aura colors. At the 35$^{th}$ meeting I said aura-sightings could help us understand other people, and moved on to one of Lynn's problems: inability to look other people in the eye. By the close of our session, she had learned how.

The vital component of Lynn's meditation sessions was the Light, and in order to use it in daily life as well as meditation, she had to "see" auras. She worked on that during our 35$^{th}$ and 36$^{th}$ meetings. To teach your child the lesson, see Building Block V.

Session 37 encouraged love of all earth's creatures with an Imaginary visit to the Peaceable Kingdom. At Session 38, on April 12, 1997, Lynn practiced breathing from her diaphragm to control her body and mind, whether awake or dreaming. Session 39 used meditation to once again stress kindness to all living things.

Lynn's father brought her to our 40th meeting on 5/3/97 so we could review the effect of a full year of meditation on her life. When I asked what her biggest problem was and whether the Light had helped her solve it, she replied: "Times are hard." Further questioning revealed she was talking about multiplication, so we reviewed the process of "over-learning" and ways of mastering multiplication tables.

Meditation 41 featured an imaginary journey to a butterfly museum that had opened in Canada. Then we compared the transformation of caterpillar to butterfly to our turning inner Light into brilliant reality.

After a summer hiatus due to Lynn's, her sister Ruth's and my rehearsals and performances of a historical play I had written, we resumed meditation on 8/8/97. A few yards upstream of the area where we staged our play, Artpark personnel and visiting Japanese artists had stretched 250 wind-socks which were shaped and painted like enormous carp, from the American bank of the Niagara River to the Canadian cliffs.

The importance of protecting the environment and the children of the world, which was symbolized by the Koinobori Festival, became the focus of our 42$^{nd}$ meditation.

Sessions 43 and 44, which took place just before Lynn started Fourth Grade, were spent visualizing success in school, and thus using the imaginary world to sharpen the senses for the real one.

The start of the school year turned Lynn hyper, but our 45$^{th}$ meditation quickly quieted her and she fell asleep. I used her nap time to fulfill a request from her Grandmother: to rehearse walking alone from her house through the back lots to the Street where her Grandmother was waiting.

Lynn brought the results of a Life Skills test to show me at our 46$^{th}$ session, on 10/4/97. She earned a 90 for describing a paragraph, a 90 on a Science quiz, and an 88 in reading. Some of her papers were starred and she achieved a respectable overall grade of 82.

Lynn arrived tired and jumpy at Session 47, but carrying a Social Studies test on which she earned 100.

Even better, she had used her experiences with the Light when she blanked out during a noisy pancake breakfast in a large public hall. Outside the building she responded to nothing until her grandfather calmly reminded her to find the Light. Within a moment, her face came alive and she returned to the break-fast and enjoyed it despite the continued noise and confusion.

The ability of my small ADD friend to handle public commotion and the excellence of her report card told me our sessions were no longer needed. But Lynn was performing once again in Nutcracker Suite at the end of Novem-ber, so her grandmother, mother and I decided to wait a couple of weeks before I informed her of the change.

Meditation sessions made her feel special and she wanted to continue, until I told her that she knew all she needed at this point in her life. Now she had to be free to use the meditations to the fullest. After some months passed, we would meet again to assess her progress. That meeting was scheduled for January of 1999.

It became a great celebration. Lynn, whose intelligence had not registered on the I.Q. scale in March of 1996, had learned how to learn. The following report cards, one from November 1997 when I told her she would have to use her meditation expertise on her own, and the last, a year after we ceased meeting, were evidence of what is possible for a child with ADD who had NEVER been medicated for the ailment.

Grade 3 Report Card 11/97 Grade 4 Report Card 11/98

| | | |
|---|---|---|
| READING | B | A- |
| MATHEMATICS | B- | B |
| SPELLING | B+ | B- |
| LANGUAGE | B | A- |
| SOCIAL STUDIES | A | B+ |
| SCIENCE | A- | A |

<u>Building Blocks of Light</u> will help your students make similar advancements in learning and behavior.

# Prelude to Chapter 3

Sigmund Freud once said that we use only 10% of our brains. But times have changed. Today, simple meditation techniques can release areas of the brain from their long suppression by the world of the five senses.

That release requires the concerted effort of a "mystic" three: Body, Mind and Spirit. Each is capable of independent action, but the real gains come from interactions of the parts. The Mind, for example, can heal the BODY of Self or others by allying with the third "mystical" component, the Spirit.

Since "Spirit," along with "God" and similar references to a Higher Power are unpopular terms in public schools, "Spirit" will thus be referred to as the "Light Within" at first, and then simply the Light. None of the three components of the Self should be omitted in attempts to improve learning. Men with brilliant minds and weak Spirit have committed some of the world's most heinous crimes. What good is intelligence when it is used for evil? And how much better for an intelligent Mind and positive Spirit to be in a healthy Body? Concerted work on all three aspects of the Self yields the greatest rewards.

The Light of Spirit is the key to showing students how to access the brain level where learning and decision making become easy and healing is possible. The beginning Building Blocks A through D will acquaint students with the necessity of the Light, while Block XYZ will allow them to transfer it to the world of the five senses.

# Chapter 3

Children who suffer from physical, mental or emotional impairment are not the only ones who need meditation. All of us do, but especially educators and parents who must deal with the "impaired." When youngsters disrupt our lives, we react angrily. Feeling our displeasure, they become increasingly difficult.

Yet children with physical, mental or emotional difficulties are not acting out of rebellion or meanness. What happens is not their fault.

Fortunately, educational authorities have started to address the situation. Numerous Guidance Counselors and Elementary School teachers are restoring order in their classrooms with Guided Imagery sessions. The results are great, but while a typical scenario - such as a quiet walk through an imaginary park - restores temporary order, many students remain outside Alpha's candy store, noses pressed to the glass.

Building Blocks of Light will show you
how to usher them into the area of consciousness where learning is a pleasure.

If you are not already a meditator, the
following pages will familiarize you with the
basic techniques.

Meditation is an ancient procedure. The
Old Testament tells of many who enjoyed the
process, starting with Abraham who "meditated
in the cool of the evening." However, the
practice was not widely accepted until the
Twentieth Century, when medical practitioners
and electrical engineers started taking notice
of Dr. Hans Berger's 1929 report of brain os-
cillations that deviated from those which occur when we use our five senses. Calling these
the Beta Waves, Berger identified their normal
rate of vibrations as 14 to 18 beats a second.

The slower waves he discovered were between 8 and 13 vibrations per second. He
called them Alpha Rhythms.[2]

Subsequent investigators and engineers
soon identified a third and fourth level of

[2] W. Gray Walter, "The Electrical Activity of the Brain" in Altered States of Awareness, San Francisco, W. H. Freeman and Company, 1972, pp. 4-13. This publication is a reprintof articles originally published in Scientific American between 1954 and 1971.

brain activity, Delta Rhythms which oscillated at between 5 and 8 vibes/sec, and the Theta Waves, below 5 pulses a second.

The next step was to trace the emergence of brain waves from birth to adulthood. Scientists concluded that in infancy Delta Rhythms dominate. These large Theta waves, below 5 vibrations per second, control deep and dreamless sleep for people of all ages.

They also discovered that around a child's first birthday the human brain emits Theta Rhythms, below 5 vibrations a second—the pattern associated with sleep and dreaming.

All brain activity is important, but Alpha waves are the key to clear thinking and healthy living. This brain pattern emerges in children who begin to build the faster than Theta waves when they are between two and three years old. These 8-13 vibrations per second Alpha Rhythms dominate until the child is 7 or a bit older. Their effects are evident. Children between the ages of three and eight acquire information in heaps and bunches with no apparent effort. Some of them can hear a television commercial once and recite it verbatim. They are avid learners, as those who deal with their endless questions will agree. This is normal, for at this time of their lives they are operating principally at the Alpha level.

Thus, it is not surprising that "going on eight years old" Lynn "found the Light" so quickly. Her dominant brain pattern allowed her to suspend the rules of the "real world" (that is, the world as perceived by the five senses). At the Alpha Level, individuals have access to a Sixth Sense and can work with what has been called Extrasensory Perception. The term ESP, so often used in the fifties and sixties, refers to what can happen at the Alpha level of consciousness. Though the acronym became part of the New Age vocabulary, there is nothing weird about the process. This brainwave is part of the human body and can be accessed easily and safely through meditation.

The meditation procedure is easy. All it takes is a fervent desire to end the turmoil in your classroom or family, a half hour of your time each day and the willingness to follow a few simple rules.

Start by seating yourself in a quiet and darkened room. If in your apartment or house is noisy, use earplugs. Sit with your spine straight, your head erect, hands resting on your thighs and feet flat on the floor.

Breath control is the key to turning off the senses—sight, sound, touch, taste and feel—which keep us in Beta. We can reach the Alpha Level—where the brain does its thinking, problem solving, etc., by counting a slow five for an inhale, three for a hold, six for an exhale, three for a hold. My usual practice, however, is to ask each person to close his eyes and imagine (s)he is entering a private elevator at the sixth floor.

Turn and face the doors, and as they close, watch the indicator above the doors. Take a deep breath and on the exhale, start your descent to the fifth floor. To ensure that, see and say its number: 5, 5, 5.

Inhale, and then exhale to 4, 4, 4.

Inhale slowly, exhale slowly to 3, 3, 3.

Inhale slowly, exhale slowly to 2, 2, 2.

Inhale slowly, exhale slowly to 1, 1, 1.

Inhale slowly, exhale slowly to B, B, B.

Your elevator doors will open and you will step out into a beam of bright light which shines on you from above.

Say: "I am now in the healthiest possible
State of Being.

"In this healthiest possible State I am
completely relaxed. If at any time a part of
me feels tense, I will tell it to relax. For a
tense neck, for example, I will whisper 'Relax
neck' or 'Relax whatever else' until my body
is comfortable.

"If at any time I feel myself coming up
out of this Healthiest Possible State of Being
(HPSB), I will take a deep breath and, as I
exhale, return to my HPSB at the Alpha Level.

"In this State, I and I alone will control my mind. No one but me will ever control
my mind.

"In this HPSB I will bring the Light that
shines down on me from above into my body by
inhaling it into my head. As I exhale, the
Light will push any aches, pains, worries,
tensions or fears down through my body and out
the soles of my feet. My next inhalation will
bring Light into my shoulders, arms and hands,
and my exhalation will drive any aches or
other troublesome feelings down through my
body and out the soles of my feet.

"I will continue inhaling to bring Light into my chest, then my abdominal region, then the hips, thighs, calves of the legs, and the feet. After each inhale, I will exhale all discomfort down through and out of my body.

"When my body is filled with Light, I will use the Light that shines down on me from above as a laser beam, and on the inhale, direct the laser of Light to any ailment I might have. The laser of Light will burn out any physical disease and as I exhale, my breath will expel the residue of the laser blast."

Repeat the exercise until your body feels comfortable. Then say a prayer of thanks to the Light of the Universe for its assistance.

Prior to bringing yourself out of this meditation, tell yourself that when you return to the Sensory World (the Beta State), your body will feel as though it is new made and in perfect working condition. Tell yourself that you are completely relaxed and will remain so the rest of your day. Tell yourself that you are filled with energy, a quiet energy which will permit you to fulfill all your responsibilities in a calm manner. Tell yourself you are filled with Joy, a Joy that will last for days.

To return to the waking State, step into your private elevator and face the doors. As you inhale, you will rise to the next floor, so help yourself to rise by seeing and saying the number of the floor.

Inhale and rise slowly to 1, 1, 1. Exhale.

Inhale and drift up to 2, 2, 2. Exhale.

Inhale and float gently up to 3, 3, 3. Exhale.

Inhale and rise softly to 4, 4, 4. Exhale.

Your elevator doors open and you step out, feeling refreshed, energized and joyous.

Note that you started down from the sixth floor, but you rise only to the fourth. There you will be at a lower level of Beta, where you can avoid the stress and strain imposed by over-reaction to the World of the Five Senses.

A short meditation such as this is all you require for now. Hereafter the Building Blocks will assist you in making whatever physical, mental or spiritual adjustments you—as well as your child—need for your comfort and advancement in the universe. If you wish to continue adult meditation exercises after you finish teaching your children the Building Blocks, you will find full instructions in my adult meditation book.[3]

"Impaired" youngsters will be especially eager to join you in meditation. You are offering what each of us yearns for: undivided attention and unconditional love. Instructions must be adjusted to their level of understanding, of course, but children under the age of eight are already operating on wavelengths that promote learning.

You will know when the meditation begins to work its magic, for your voice will lose its sharp and cranky edge and become soft and loving. And that is necessary, for your goal is Unconditional Love.

For that, at present, we must look to meditation techniques that feature a single concept and two personal requirements.

The vital "concept" is the belief that each of us is needed and wanted in the world. Children often lack that assurance, and the

---

[3] (Margaret) Sanders G. Laurie and Melvin J. Tucker, Centering Your Guide to Inner Growth. Rochester, Vermont: Destiny Books, 1993.

situation worsens for those with physical, mental or emotional disabilities. Youngsters such as these can become disruptive and so incur the displeasure of their elders. The resultant criticisms and reprimands prevent their building self-confidence. Their alienation from family soon extends to alienation from the greater world.

Even children raised with loving care crave "acceptance" beyond the confines of their homes. For a time "gifts" from Santa Claus and the Easter Bunny can assure little ones of their importance to the universe. But their sense of "belonging" fades with the holidays. As with all humans, children need a greater assurance. One that comes solely from belief in a Divine Power. From a belief in goodness and rightness. From learning that the Light of a caring Universe pours down on each of us because we are important to It. From knowing the Light will guide us, protect us, and help heal our wounds.

Many adults resist these concepts. Nonetheless, anyone involved in meditations that combine spiritual elements with techniques suited to his level of comprehension will gain

47

greater respect for self and the rest of the universe.

My usual adult meditation had to be simplified for Lynn. And her response, since—at the start—she was within the age bracket when the Alpha Level is strongest, was immediate. While adults may require three or four classes before they find and become comfortable with "the Light of the Universe" Lynn succeeded in a bit over a minute. And the Light made it possible for her to overcome the worst aspects of her Attention Deficit Disorder and begin to learn what her classroom peers had already mastered.

You can do the same for your students IF you abide by two rules. The first is UNCONDITIONAL LOVE. No matter how much you may hate your students' behavior (due to their conditions) in meditation you must see only their Spiritual selves.

The second rule is DETACHMENT. In meditation we must confine our teaching to Spiritual matters. We must avoid talking about OUR religion. We must forget OUR egos, OUR self-interests, OUR conclusions, and think only of the youngsters'. We teach the process and

stand back and let them form their own concepts and fashion their own beliefs. We permit
them the freedom of thought and expression we
claim for ourselves.

We'll discuss this again and again. For
now, if you agree to these requirements,
you're ready for specific instructions. We
shall begin with suggestions for you, and follow with the exercises you will introduce to
the needy children you teach.

We call these exercises Building Blocks
of Light. The initial ones, marked A, B, C, D,
and XYZ, are the foundations of child meditation. You will use them always, adding other
blocks which will be discussed in later chapters.

Suggestions for your teaching will be
preceded by bullets (e.g.: o).

Helpful information included in BUILDING
BLOCKs will be set off by [brackets] to dis-
tinguish it from instruction you give directly
to your group.

Let us begin.

**PREPARING YOURSELF FOR TEACHING MEDITATION:**

o Provide yourself with a loose leaf notebook so you can keep track of what you have covered in each session and the possible results of your teaching.

o Choose one or a group of up to four children in your classroom who have serious learning problems or who cause disruption. Counselors may have time for one-on-one sessions with an individual student, but District budgets may make it necessary for an educator to teach this method to four students at a time.

o Set aside an hour for the initial session, and meet with your group in a quiet room with dim light. If the room has a phone, unplug it. Leave the rest of your class in care of another educator.

o Before inviting your group into the room, calm yourself with a breathing exercise. Inhale and hold your breath as you say "1-relaxing; 2-relaxing; 3-relaxing." Exhale to "1-relaxing; 2-relaxing; 3-relaxing." Repeat for seven full breaths or until you are at ease. Prepare to speak slowly and calmly. If your meditation students annoy you in any way

during the session, know that it is their condition which causes the misbehavior. Breathe
slowly until you regain your serenity before
gently correcting them. Praise them often during your session, by soft word and loving tone
of voice.

**BUILDING BLOCKS OF LIGHT**

**BUILDING BLOCK A:** Tell your group that
they and you are going to play a game. If they
resist or are restless, tell them they must
breathe slowly in order to play. Ask them to
inhale while you count to three, then exhale
for a count of three. Do this until each of
your students, like you, is composed.

**BUILDING BLOCK B:** In the softest and
calmest voice possible, say all of you will
close your eyes and go on a search. Tell them:
"Take a deep breath, and see yourself inside
your throat. Oh, how warm and comfortable it
is going down in the dark. Your chest's dark,
too. But not for long. You're going to find
the spark of life within you. It is the Light
of the Spirit of the Universe. You'll have to

search for it, though. It's tiny. Most people find just a pinprick of Light. At first. Take your time and look for it. It's there, waiting for you to find it. Let me know when you do."

{Children between the ages of four and eight usually find the Light within two minutes. If your charges take longer, say: "You're doing just fine. The Light's there, but we may need to coax it out. And you'll be glad you did, for this Light inside you is the key to learning." (Continue with Block C}.

**BUILDING BLOCK C:** Tell them softly, "Do you know that, along with the Light within, you have a Light that shines on you from above? This is also the Light of the Universe, and we'll bring it down into our chests. Let's do it now. Taking deep breaths, we'll bring the Light through the tops of our heads and down into our chests. We'll breathe out any darkness in there. Breathe in, and the Light will flash down into our chests, find the pinpoint of Light inside us and turn the pinpoint into blazing Light. There now. My chest is filled with Light. How about yours? Wonderful. You did that well. Fast, too. I'm proud of you."

**BUILDING BLOCK D:** Say: "Let's begin by talking about what the Light is going to do for you. In finding this Light, you have opened the doors to learning. When you reach this brain level, you will understand everything that is going on around you, everything you read, everything you see on a TV screen. You will understand what you hear, as well as anything else that comes to you through the senses of touch, taste and feel. Even better, the Light will help you decide how to make decisions about or otherwise react to this information that floods into our minds from the world of the five senses. On reaching this brain level, you have also been given the key to body health. Later we'll use the Light to learn, but today the Light of the Universe will flush any aches, pains, worries, or fears from your body. Since your head and chest are already filled with Light, breathe out any bad feelings from your arms and hands and make room for pure Light. With your eyes closed, look down into your chest and see how bright it's become. It even "feels light" and might float away if it weren't attached to your hips and legs. Now, my friends, breathe out any bad feelings in your abdomen and hips, and breathe in the Light. Do the same for your legs and feet. That's wonderful. You did so well that you're light enough to float into the air with me and go on a vacation.

"We can go anyplace you like, for your mind can—and should—control your body.

{Take them to a vacation spot of their choice. But make it a peaceful place. Even an exciting themepark like Disney World can be peaceful and joyous if presented in the right way. Bring in all the details of your trip. Take your time with this part of the exercise, which is stretching children's minds as well as teaching them how to use their brains to control their bodies}.

**BUILDING BLOCK XYZ:** {The trip finished, lavish praise on them for being so attentive and quick to respond}. Add: "You will open your eyes soon. When you do, you will be relaxed and happy. You will carry your Light with you the rest of the day and all the night. If you become excited, close your eyes and find the Light. It will help you while you're awake.

Good. You've worked hard and I'm proud of you. Now let's open our eyes, feeling rested and relaxed, and go rejoin the rest of our class."

o You have just introduced your students to Blocks of Light. Blocks A, B, C, D, and XYZ are the foundation for Blocks of Light E through W (which will be introduced in later chapters). Use Blocks which will describe imaginary trips after presenting difficult Blocks. As you continue, block by block, you and your students will learn to cope with their learning disabilities and other problems. As they improve, you will understand the process and your importance to it.

o If at any time your students become over-excited or out of control during the school day, stop them and ask in a quiet voice that they find their Light. If that does not relax them enough, ask them to breathe in and out as you count by threes. Reinforce the lesson of the meditation exercise by adding it to their regular routine, for learning becomes easy when people turn off the world of the five senses and open their minds to Light.

o Throughout your day, practice breathing slowly yourself. In doing so you will remain calm and collected, and be able to temper the turmoil caused by your students' conditions.

o Be easy on yourself. Do not punish your body by being angry or frustrated over circumstances that are currently beyond your control. A quiet, calm atmosphere is needed if children are to improve. And that will happen if you persist in teaching matters of the Light. Chances are that your students—like many children who are physically, mentally or emotionally burdened—feel unloved and unwanted by the great world.

Knowing they harbor "the Light within" will raise their self-esteem and increase their desire to contribute to the world's well-being.

# Prelude to Chapter 4

Building Blocks E and F employ the concept of "As Above, So Below" to show the connectedness of each student's Spirit-Mind-Body to the Universe, the Earth and to other humans. In trying to improve students' lives we deal with complex problems: poor self-image and often harsh realities of their home\school lives. And the heavier the load, the more the child misbehaves. The sole way to change them is to give them a sense of "belonging" and the "self confidence" that comes from being praised for doing something right—even if you have to work day and night to find that rare "something." Though it may take time to "heal the wounds inflicted by other people," your efforts will be richly rewarded.

Students who realize their interconnectedness with the universe will work hard to earn your approval.

# Chapter 4

"Impaired" youngsters will be especially eager to join you in meditation. You are offering what each of us yearns for: undivided attention and unconditional love. Instructions must be adjusted to their level of understanding, of course, but children under the age of eight are already operating on wavelengths that promote learning.

You will know when the meditation begins to work its magic, for your voice will lose its sharp and cranky edge and become soft and loving. And that is necessary, for your goal is Unconditional Love.

For that, at present, we must look to meditation techniques that feature a single concept and two personal requirements.

The vital "concept" is the belief that each of us is needed and wanted in the world. Children often lack that assurance, and the situation worsens for those with physical, mental and emotional disabilities. Youngsters with these ailments can become disruptive and so incur the displeasure of their elders. The resultant criticisms and reprimands prevent their building self-confidence. Their alienation from family soon extends to alienation from the greater world.

Even children raised with loving care crave "acceptance" beyond the confines of their homes. For a time "gifts" from Santa Claus or the Easter Bunny assure little ones of their importance to the universe. But their sense of "belonging" fades with the holidays. As with all humans, children need a greater assurance. One that comes solely from belief in a Divine Power.

From a belief in goodness and rightness. From learning that the Light of a caring Universe pours down on each of us because we are important to It. From knowing the Light will guide us, protect us, and help heal our wounds.

Some adults resist these concepts. Nonetheless, anyone who uses meditation to combine spiritual elements with techniques suited to his level of comprehension will gain greater respect for self and the rest of the universe.

If your initial mediation seemed to have no effect on your students, take heart. Give yourself time to see them as beloved by the Universe. Give them however long they need to grasp the spiritual tools of meditation. This is the beginning of a new and better world for both of you.

Since you cannot give more than you have, seek to know better so you will give better. To that end, before you sit down with them for your second meditation, consider the following:

o You will be worthy of this responsibility as long as you have their well-being at heart. Though you may not have taught meditation before, you are a trained educator and will know what to do. Your work on their behalf will be the most important therapy of their lives, for you are showing them how to use the Body, Mind and Spirit of their unique Selves.

o In meditation sessions, lay aside your role as authority figure. You can best reach your students by showing an interest in them and their thoughts. Gently, and with as much humor as possible, work on their problems.

One of Lynn's was her short attention span. We started to s-t-r-e-t-c-h that out by asking for and softly insisting on details.

The least detail merits praise, for children are the same as us. We like approval and will go out of our way to get more. Be lavish with your compliments. Avoid criticism of any sort. This is bonding time, and love is the tie that binds.

Save your authoritative stance for regular classroom teaching.

o In meditation, avoid negative phrases (e.g.: You will not misbehave. Or, You are being bad again). Use positive words (e.g.: You are behaving perfectly. You are the best child I know. Thank you.) Speak softly, confidently, as though what you want for your students has ALREADY HAPPENED. In your instructions, indicate the desired action is here and now, not in the future. These instructions will reach their Subconscious minds so they can begin to make the desired improvements.

o As you teach, search for ways to build the children's self-esteem. Let them know they are treasured members of your class and have unique abilities. If their abilities appear limited to you, at this point, refrain from saying so.

o Tell them they are persons first and foremost, as they will discover as they continue working with Universal Light. Say that despite any disabilities they may have, they have the **A**-bility to experience life, earn the love and respect of other people, and become fulfilled and successful adults.

o Begin on a small scale. Assure them of your love and say you want what is best for them. Ask them what they can do to make the classroom a happier place. Write down their answers in your log. Further, ask them what they can do to help at home. Suggest chores suitable to their ages and let them choose.

o Say it is all right to make mistakes. Everybody does. But smart people think about their failures and find ways to turn them into triumphs.

o Expect the best. In my years of teaching, I welcomed freshmen to my English courses by saying they were all bright people or they would not be in college. All could earn A's if they used their time and energy to find new slants on old topics and revised each of their fourteen essays until they were mistake-free. Some students had to rewrite essays twelve

times before they reached the C (college com-
petency) level, but even some of them Aced the
course. The reason? People live up to your ex-
pectations of them.

So will your students. But consider their
welfare before you decide what you want for
them. Temper ambition with reason. To expect a
paraplegic to become an Olympic track star,
for instance, would be pushing. It may be possible—who is to say?—if a child desires it
with all his/her heart. Encourage your group
to honestly assess their conditions and set
their own goals. Grant them the freedom and
support to do so and they will make you proud.

With these thoughts in mind, and using
the techniques outlined in chapter 2 (that is,
choosing a quiet spot and relaxing, etc.), you
are ready to teach your class its second lesson in meditation.

o Softly and gently tell them you love
them and are proud to have such fine people in
your classes. Tell them you regret having to
reprimand them, at times, for their behavior.
Say that the disruption of the classroom hurts
you as much as it does them, for you know that
up to now they have been unable to help them-

selves. But you think that working with the Light could change you as well as them. Say all of you will start by trying to slow everyone's breathing. Lead them here in slow-breathing for at least three breaths. Continue to seven—more if necessary—until both of you are relaxed.

## BUILDING BLOCKS OF LIGHT

Begin the meditation with Building Blocks A through D.

**BUILDING BLOCK E:** Remind your group that the Light of Spirit, like that of the sun, shines down from above and surrounds them with Light. They can use this Light for Healing. Ask them to see themselves standing still on a green lawn and growing roots out of the bottoms of their feet.

Say: "Do you see how bright the Light is around you? Do you feel Its warmth, especially at the top of your head? Good. Now, take a deep breath and bring the Light from above down into your head. As you let your breath out, the Light will push any worries, troubles, aches or other bad stuff down through your body to the soles of your feet. Then the bad stuff will go out the bottoms of your feet and into the ground."

Continue the exercise, inhaling the Light and exhaling the "dark" for shoulders, arms and hands; chest; abdomen and hips; thighs; lower legs; feet. When done, tell them to use three inhalations to bring the Light into their entire bodies and flush out any remaining problems. Congratulate everyone on being filled with Light, and tell them all of you will repeat this exercise often.

Explain that: "Though accidents can cause immediate injury to the body, illnesses often build up over time. But whether an ailment is recent or of long-standing, our bodies don't heal immediately, except in rare instances. Usually—because bodies are busy doing their daily work—it takes days to heal a small cut, weeks for a big cut. Recovery from an illness sometimes takes months. But the healing Light of the Universe does restore bone and tissue, so we have to keep working at it.

Continue with: "However, there is a way to speed up the healing process, and that is to share the Light with other people."

O Follow up with:

**BUILDING BLOCK F:** Tell them that while they are standing on the grass, the roots which have grown out of their feet into the earth below will start going deeper, as well as stretching out in all directions to become en-tangled with the roots of other students in the classroom.

Say: "This might sound like a crazy idea, but it isn't. Not at all, and I'll tell you why. Suppose we are facing a range of mountains with sharp peaks, and we look up at them and see that mists are rising from the valley where we stand, and running up the mountain sides. Thus, when we look at the peaks, it ap-pears that each is a separate mountain—just as it appears we are separate people. But when the winds come up and drive the clouds and mists away, we see that each mountain is part of its neighbor. As are we.

"Now you know that you're part of your parents. The color of your eyes or skin, the size of your nose, the curve of your mouth—these are family traits. But you're also part of your cousins, your neighbors, everyone in this school, county, state...Each of us is part of the whole—the entire Universe! And our bodies each contain the same elements, and in the same proportions, as Earth and possibly the rest of the Universe.

"Knowing every one of us is part of the Whole, we can help heal each other as well as ourselves. So right now, feel the roots from your feet dig deeper and wider into the earth beneath you and entangle with other roots. See yourself as a tree in the forest, and feel the strength and safety which comes from having roots entangled with other trees so none will blow over in a wild storm. That done, bring the Light down into the top of your head, down through your body, and into the roots of your feet so it can flash across to join the Light of the rest of us. Be calm, be confident, and know that the exchange of Light can and will heal our ailments as well as those of the people we share it with. Close your eyes and check your own body to see if you don't feel better. Even if you're in perfect health, acting as a conduit for the Light will make you feel great. I am proud of you for having shared the Light with others. It will help you

in so many ways. You'll see when you get far-
ther along.

"Right now I have a favor to ask. All of
us are just beginning to learn about the Light
and if we talk about it before we have proof
that it works, other people (even our families,
maybe) might think we're crazy.

"You see, people who have not experienced
the Light do not know what It can do. If It's
a new idea to them, they may even fear it
enough to tell you It's evil. That's not true.
The Light that shines within us and down on
our heads is pure goodness. It always has been
and will ever be.

"Our Light comes from the Universe. Some
say it comes from "God," but because we're not
talking about religion, we call it the Good of
the Universe. Our Light comes directly from
this Good, as does the Light of all inhabi-
tants of earth. Most of our world's religions
believe there is at least one other type of
Light giver besides a God. They call them Angels. Around the globe, people of various religions believe every human is under the pro-
tection of his or her own Guardian Angel.
Would you like to find out if it's so?

"Good. Now close your eyes and ask your Guardian to stand at your right shoulder. Your eyes still closed, turn your head and see what your Guardian looks like. Is it a young man- or young woman? It may be hard to tell, for both wear white robes and have long hair. But, usually, boys have male Angels and girls, female Angels. Ask his or her name and repeat it when you thank the Light for taking care of you. Also tell your Guardian we've used up our time for Light work, but you will call for him (her) as soon as possible so you can become better acquainted.

Tell your students: "It's best not to talk to other people about the Light or your Guardian until you, yourself, become better acquainted with both and know what they can do and have done for you. When the proof is in, you can shout it to the world."

o Conclude your session with Building Block XYZ.

o The Building Blocks of this session are among the most important ones of the series. You have undertaken this method of behavior modification in order to improve the lives of your students, their families, and their schoolmates. If, as a meditation teacher, you remain detached from your own beliefs or convictions and exhibit Unconditional Love for your group, you will succeed.

Proof that you are teaching them to be positive thinkers will be found in succeeding chapters. The Light heightens moral and ethical sensibilities. The Building Blocks will help you and your child develop or increase your Spiritual awareness. The Light would not allow it otherwise.

o When you become comfortable with teaching meditation, set aside time to teach it two days a week. Frequent meditations will help your group improve faster, and all improvement will increase their ability to learn.

o But a word of caution. During your meditation sessions you will strive to be relaxed and calm. Try now to carry these attitudes over to your daily association with your class. There, as a teacher, calmly identify what you require of students in the way of conduct and behavior. Do NOT be permissive. Youngsters need to know you are strong and firm, and that they can depend on you to live up to the ideals you have been teaching them in meditation.

# Prelude to Chapter 5

As with everyone else, young children need to see results in order to Believe. Building Blocks G and H, therefore, introduce your students to their emotions and show them how to rid themselves of those which can make them ill.

Block I, a trip over a rainbow, is their reward for working so hard to improve their inner selves.

A more tangible gift might be a small, inexpensive rainbow decal for each Student—or a small packet of gold coins. Think of this NOT as buying their good Will, but as thanks for their improvement in behavior. You want them to like the Building Block technique, for you'll be using it soon to increase their abilities to learn.

# Chapter 5

While a college degree is required for teachers, you do not need that or other educational credits to show another human how to find the Spirit. All that's required is Unconditional Love for the individuals you are teaching and the kind of Detachment which permits you to teach ONLY matters of the Spirit.

Consider the sun that blesses the earth with its light. Once called a god, the sun now represents the order and beneficence of the universe. It is a symbol of SPIRIT, and ignores specific doctrines and personal beliefs. Trust in Spirit and allow your students to learn from IT, not you, during meditation sessions.

Save all discussions about habits, morals, etc. for day-in-day-out educational sessions.

Trust in Spirit to keep your roles of meditation-teacher and subject-teacher separate and distinct.

If, having done that, you still feel inadequate, teach yourself adult meditation with Centering Your Guide to Inner Growth (see Ch. 3 footnote).

If your students' disabilities have thrown your life into disorder, turn that around by bonding with them in meditation. Healing will follow: theirs from learning how to behave and yours from their doing so.

Steady improvement is desired, of course, but be prepared for fits and starts. Students may revert to former behavior patterns as the stress of a new school year looms, or they become excited about a birthday, religious holiday, a performance or our annual "show of shows," Halloween. Disturbances in family routine may also cause trouble.

I feared Lynn might be in for a bad time when she learned her mother was leaving her and her sisters with a babysitter for a week. Lynn adores everyone in her family, but most of all, her mother. Fortunately, just two sessions of "working with the Light" showed her how to be "a perfect angel" during her mother's absence.

o Beginning the meditation program early in a semester will prepare you for handling whatever problems arise as your students grow. But early or late, begin. The greatest thing you can give another person is the trust in a higher power that leads to confidence in self. Building Blocks helps children become self-confident, so after you have covered the opening exercises (Blocks A through D) continue with the following.

**BUILDING BLOCK G:** Say: "The Light from Spirit is a healing Light, class. If any part of us is not working perfectly, we can use the Light to cure it. That includes the Mind, but let's start with the body first. With your eyes still closed, look up and see the Light become thin as a stick of chalk and just as white. Now, as you breathe the Light down through the top of your head, see it flash—like a laser beam—right to a spot that needs healing. Watch the white beam dry up the sick cells. Look at them. Those bad cells are drying up and flaking off, so you can breathe them out through your nose if they're in the upper part of your body, or out the soles of your feet if they're in your lower body. Very good. Now, if you have a spot that needs healing, work on it at home. Right before you go to bed is a good time. Sit with your spine straight, feet on the floor, hands on lap, and bring the Light down to the troublesome spot and watch it do Its healing.

The Light can improve any part of ourselves. What we call the Self has three parts: Body, Mind, and Spirit. The Light can cure any of these and right now we're going to use it to feel better about ourselves."

O Move ahead then to **Building Block H.**


**BUILDING BLOCK H**

O Ask your students if they have any problems that bother them or if they get mad sometimes. If they say no, ask each of them to remember a time when they were angry with someone. Say, "How do you feel inside yourself now, students? Is anger burning your chest? Is it flaring up into your head and making you want to say or do something to get even? That's what it does to most people.

"But getting mad hurts you more than the other person. He can ignore our anger and walk away, but our bodies are still hurting. Like all bad feelings, anger poisons our insides and dims our Light. And that's stupid, because bad feelings don't last. Let me show you.

"Think about the best present you ever got. Why did you want it and were you happy when you got it? Tell me about it, each of you. We'll start with the person on my left.

When all have complied, say: "See there? One minute you were so mad that you felt you had a hot ball inside you. Thinking about the gift you received made you feel good. That's because feelings come and go. They're visitors who drop by now and again. But feelings like anger, hate, and jealousy are bad visitors. We don't have to invite them in. If we do, they'll make us miserable. They'll certainly dim our Light, at least for a little while.

"So what can we do when we start feeling mean? We should look inside ourselves and see our bright Light turn into dark red stuff that's churning around in our chests and making us feel awful. That stuff's not part of us. It's visiting, that's all.

So we get rid of it. We turn it off—flip a switch and shut it off like a TV or Stereo. Instead of that ugly red mess that was in our bodies, we find Light—beautiful, soothing Light that brings us every good thing."

Repeat **BUILDING BLOCK H** for several meditations. Your students may not like it as well
as the imaginary journey blocks, but they need
it to overcome fits of temper or other emotions which result from their disabilities.
Also, any time a meditation students throws a
temper tantrum in regular class, give him a
time-out to get rid of his "bad visitors."

o In regular classroom time as well as
meditation, PRAISE THEM, PRAISE THEM for even
the smallest improvements in behavior modification.

O Use the following **BUILDING BLOCK** to af-
firm the uplifting quality of the Light. A
visit to a rainbow, which began with Lynn, is
one I have used since with other youngsters
who have learning disabilities. They adore it.
So might your students.

Use your own region for the story. Start
the rainbow wherever you like, but bring it
down in a nearby park or other grassy spot.

**BUILDING BLOCK I**: Tell your meditators:
"You've worked hard on your exercises and deserve some fun. What say we fill ourselves
with Light and fly up into the sky to look for

a rainbow? We're most apt to find one when the sun's low in the sky. Tell me when you're Light enough to take off. You ready so soon? Wonderful. Let's go. Up, up, through the roof of our building and on up through the clouds. Look around now. We need a storm cloud. Nothing too big, just one that will drop enough rain for the sun to shine through and form our rainbow. There's a possible cloud near the horizon. Let's zip over and see if it's one we want.

"Oh yes. Look down there. A cloud let loose its rain, sure enough. There's a rainbow. A real beauty. Let's zoom down to its starting place."

o Continue the imaginary journey by asking your students what colors they see in the rainbow. If they are old enough to understand, add information about the refraction of light which forms the brilliant band. But keep your informational lecture short, to avoid their losing interest.

o Begin your walk up and across the rainbow. Use steps as I did with Lynn, or treat it as a gentle slope, but do add railings for the children to hang onto.

o As you mount the rainbow, say: "Look below us, everyone, and tell us what you see. People? Cars? Look how small they're becoming. Oh—crowds are gathering at street corners and looking up at our rainbow. They don't see us, though. That's because our Light is mixing with the light of the rainbow."

o At the top of the rainbow, comment on how small the buildings, cars and people seem to be from high in the air. Point out places of interest such as your house, the school-house, a park or playground, and other special sites. Then start down the bridge of light.

Tell them: "Hey, the rainbow ends in the park. I don't see people—unless you want to count that tiny figure in green at the foot of the rainbow a person. I suspect he's the Lep-rechaun who's guarding the gold at rainbow's end. What do you think?

{Give students time for each to express an opinion. If you have a 'quiet' student, ask him a question about the Leprechaun.}

Add: "Oh my. He's coming up the rainbow to meet us. He looks grumpy. He's waving his arms and shouting at us to go back. He says the rainbow's dissolving and isn't safe to walk on. Humph. It looks fine to me. What do you think, class?

"Yes. It's safe. The Leprechaun knows it, too. He thought he could scare us off. Since his plan didn't work, he's backing up. Fast. Come on, let's see if we can beat him to the ground. No. He had too good a start on us. You see where he ran? Over near the picnic benches. He's trying to lure us away from the end of the rainbow, I expect. That's because he has something hidden under the rainbow's end. Lift the colored hem off the grass to find it. Good. Pull it out now. Sure and begorry, it's a pot of gold. It's yours now. The Leprechaun doesn't like having to give it up, but that's the rule. Whoever finds it at rainbow's end gets to keep it. Everyone will get an equal share, so pick up your gold coins, thank the Leprechaun and we'll start home. We won't return over the rainbow bridge unless you want to. We're filled with Light, so we can fly home. When we get there, put your imaginary gold beside your bed. You want it near, for anytime you become tired or anxious or fearful, you can pull out a gold coin and spend it on feeling better."

o Pack your story with as many personal details as possible, and conclude your jaunt as your students choose: re-crossing the rainbow or flying directly home.

o End your session with **BUILDING BLOCK XYZ.**

o Purchase bags of thin chocolates wrapped as gold coins for your meditation students.[4]

o A present such as this will show them that you're pleased with their progress. For lasting effect, any gift should relate to a journey in the Light. Use your own increased awareness of life to look around stores and find items you can buy for change. Expensive gifts might make your students forget what they've learned in the Light. Cost is not the object. Appropriateness is. Your gifts should build bridges from the imaginary worlds you visit during meditation to the world of the five senses. A week after a meditation that involved angels, I gave Lynn her first soap

---

[4] Net bags of chocolate wrapped as gold coins can be found in drug stores and Five and Tens besides candy stores, especially before the December holidays.

angel. The rainbow meditation was reinforced by rainbow decals presented two weeks apart. The first pot of gold came a month afterward. Do not spoil the novelty by giving rewards at every session. If you decide to give them, once a month is enough.

    o Repeat the rainbow walk during subsequent meditations if your students ask for it.

# Prelude to Chapter 6

Student Transformation occurs faster when efforts are applied equally to the Inner and Outer Selves. Prepare for this by starting a log that identifies the individual problems of their lives and your "wish-list" for improvements.

In **Block J,** you will teach your students how to improve their day to day "living time" by deciding what they want in life and then "foreseeing good" in order to achieve it. The tool is visualization, for what people consistently FORESEE IS WHAT THEY GET.

In meditation you are showing children how to use Spirit to direct their Minds and their Minds how to control their Bodies. Slow learners are in desperate need of such control. Faulty linkage between brain cells and nerve endings may make it difficult for them to concentrate.

The Body seems to be out of touch with the Mind and Spirit. But this can be changed. All can improve their conditions or even cure them—by using the spark of life and Light implanted within by Spirit.

o Tell your students they can summon the Light by just thinking about it or by closing their eyes a moment. Congratulate them on being so good and working so hard during your meditation sessions.

o That done, we can proceed to the educator's major goal— **Building Block K**—which will teach slow learners how to navigate on the informational highway. The project had to wait for students to feel comfortable with and confident about the workings of Body/Mind/Spirit, and you had important information about successful mind-training techniques.

Here, in this chapter, is the technique that took my ADHD meditator out of a 12-1-1 class into regular classrooms where she earns some C's, several B's and occasional A's.

You, of course, will have to determine your students' needs and present the material in simple ways until they learn to trust their expanded brain power.

# Chapter 6

The next step in successfully teaching meditation is to list the specific problems of each mentally or neurologically disabled child. Begin by identifying students who are:

Slow to develop either physically or mentally.

Frequently frustrated.

Prone to irritability.

Incapable of following requests or orders.

Short on attention-span and thus unable to complete most tasks.

Easily distracted, even when trying to concentrate.

Incapable of blocking out irrelevant stimuli. (At the least noise or movement, does he/she leave the business at hand and rush to investigate?)

Careless and destructive of own and others' belongings.

Accident prone, due to inattention to danger. (Darts across the street without checking traffic?)

Loud, unmannerly or disruptive. (Shouts out wrong answers in class or makes inappropriate remarks?)

Highly sensitive to other people's reactions?

O Pull out your loose-leaf journal and begin a new page for each student. Across the top of the page write SYMPTOMS on the left, TYPICALLY OCCUR at mid-page, and DESIRED BEHAVIOR on the right. Under Symptoms, jot down those traits which your student exhibits. Add any other symptoms that apply.

O Number the symptoms in order of importance to you, then fill in the second column of your log with pertinent information. For instance, the symptom "frequently frustrated" might appear "when we have visitors in class." Build your wish-list of desired behaviors in the third column. When your records of everyone's symptoms and occurrences and your desires are complete, get to work on changing their negative behavior.

*Margaret Laurie*

O Ask your students what they think they can do in conscious life to help themselves change. Record their replies in your log to guide you to the Blocks they need to achieve their goals.

**BUILDING BLOCKS OF LIGHT**

o Tell your students they will begin by tackling something that will help them learn. Suggest all write a schedule for getting ready for school in the morning. Tell them that you will later sit down with each of them to discuss what they need to do to "clear the decks for learning." A typical schedule for a youngster in the Elementary Grades could include:

Rising at a specified time in the morning.

Washing and dressing oneself quickly in clothes they put out the previous night.

Finishing breakfast by a certain time.

Putting on outerwear, picking up books and lunch (Or lunch money) and getting to the bus stop before the School Bus arrives.

Explain that they must do all this on their own, without help or prodding by adults. Successful students will receive a good grade for their good work. Then, if they like, they can add more tasks and earn more rewards.

Continue student conferences until each meditation student has his/her own assignment. If you have over four participants, however, you may need the temporary assistance of a parent or other reliable volunteer.

Begin your session as usual, with **BUILD-ING BLOCKS A-D: BUILDING BLOCK J:** Tell them: "Find your Light, everyone, so It can help you "walk-through" your morning schedule. First, pretend someone's made a movie of you doing all these things right. Then see yourself on a movie or TV screen waking up, getting out of bed in the morning, washing up and brushing your teeth, putting on clothes you laid out the night before—or whatever else you agreed to do. See yourself smile at everyone as you eat your breakfast, put on your outer-wear, then pick up your books and lunch or lunch money. View yourself wishing everyone a fine day as you head out the door to the school bus stop, where you will meet your friends."

O If anyone says he/she has no friends, tell them the Light will help them make some. You will give them a Building Block for that purpose later. Now all should fill themselves with the Light so they can begin to learn easily in school.

Tell them: "Each of you can summon the Light by closing your eyes and thinking about it. Ohh, you're doing a fine job, class. Congratulations of being so good and working so hard during meditation. And because you've made such progress, we may be able to set aside time for shorter but more frequent meditations. Shorter exercises will allow for more repetition and should be more helpful to all of us than a single hour a week. More fun, too."

O {Use **Block XYZ** to close **Block** J. Although **Blocks J and K** are meant to be taught in the same meditation period, you may wish to give your students a simplified version of the following information first. That done, re-enter with **A and B** to ensure students will be breathing slowly during **BLOCK K** coverage. }

O Visualization is a powerful tool used by Olympic contenders and other athletes. Modern techniques which employ relaxation and visualization were pioneered by three physicians: Dr. Georgi Lozanov, a native of Bulgaria, Dr. Johannes H. Schultz of Germany, and Dr. Alfonso Caycedo of Spain. Though they achieved similar results in teaching people how to learn easily, the titles of their methods differ. Lozanov's technique was called Suggestology; Schultz's, Autogenic Training; and Caycedo's, Sophrology.

O Ostrander and Schroder's <u>Superlearning</u> relates the success of one of the methods:

> For retarded and disabled children, results have been amazing. In Madrid, pediatrician Dr. Mariano Espinosa has used Caycedo's sophrology training system on problem children from all over Spain and North and South America.

> Experts were astonished by what they saw at his institute.

> Retarded youngsters with severe motor incoordination were performing sophrology physical exercises with extraordinary skill; moreover, after several

months of training body/mind as one, their IQ's had soared.

Dr. Espinosa was awarded the international gold medal in pediatrics in 1974 for his achievements with sophrology.[5]

o Though Suggestology and Sophrology use relaxed concentration to link mind and body so that learning becomes easier, they do so in different ways. Suggestology relaxes practitioners with slow music, and Sophrology uses breath control. Verbal instruction follows in both cases.

O Dr. Schultz's Autogenic Training achieves mind/body linkage through exercise. The method, as Dr. A. G. Odessky explained in a Russian publication in 1971, "develops people's ability to control consciously their various physiological processes, for example, to control digestion, breathing, blood circulation, metabolism, and also to control emotions, moods, and sharpen attention."[6]

O Experts combine Autogenics and Sophrology to teach relaxation, body control, posi-

---

[5] Sheila Ostrander and Lynn Schroeder with Nancy Ostrander, <u>Superlearning.</u> New York: Delta, 1980, p. 137.
[6] Ostrander, Schroeder, Ostrander, pp.163-164

tive affirmations and visualization to athletes preparing for Olympic competition. Swiss
skiers whose teams were not distinguishing themselves were taught these techniques. Results
were immediate. In the 1972 Winter Olympics,
three of the four competitors won medals. At
the 1972 Winter Olympics, three more Swiss
skiers became medalists.[7] Since then, athletes
all over the world have found the "winning
edge" by visualizing perfection in motion and
then, in competition, allowing their mind/body
to perform. In short, <u>What You Foresee is What
You Get.</u>

　　o In teaching meditation, you do the
same. Show children how to use Spirit to direct their Minds, and their Minds will control
their Bodies. People with neurological disorders like ADD and other mental deficiencies
are in desperate need of such control. Faulty
linkages between brain cells and nerve endings
make it difficult for them to concentrate. Their
Bodies seem to be out of touch with their
Minds and Spirit. But this can be changed. All
can improve their conditions—or even cure them

---

[7]Ostrander, Shroeder, Ostrander, p. 153.

—by using the spark of life and Light implanted within us.

**BUILDING BLOCKS OF LIGHT.** In listening to your instructions, your students may have speeded up their breathing, so begin anew with **Blocks A and B**.

**BUILDING BLOCK K:** Tell them: "This time each of you will see yourself on your mental movie screen sitting, as usual, in our classroom. Watch yourself on your screen, and see yourself understanding everything that I or another teacher tells you, as well as everything you read, see or otherwise experience. You are at the healthiest possible state of being. This means you are at ease, and need only to relax, breathe slowly, and let the Light do its healing work on your brain. Remember," WHAT YOU FORESEE IS WHAT YOU'LL GET, and this puts success within your reach.

Add that: "In everyday life, when we're using our five senses, we live by clock and calendar. You know how it is—you must be ready to leave the house in time to catch the school bus or otherwise get to school on time. Past, present and future loom large as we attempt to organize our busy lives.

In meditation we must put aside such limiting notions. To our Spirit and our Subconscious Self, the sole time is NOW. By opening our Minds to learning and our Bodies to cures, we must see our desires as having come to pass. We shall turn 'maybe someday' into 'I am now' through visualization. When you see yourselves on your movie screens as having achieved your goals, your Subconscious Selves will start to bring it to pass."

Tell your students: "When people speak about time, they often mean the 'Past, present, and future.' But each of us needs to focus on just ONE time—NOW. The past is gone. The future is the tomorrow you dreamed about yesterday. This moment, this hour is all any of us has. Be HERE NOW to make the most of it. You'll start by closing your eyes and imagining you are watching yourselves on your own large screen. We shall call it "a mental movie screen." On this screen "WHAT YOU FORESEE IS WHAT YOU'LL GET" so allow only good things to happen on your screen.

O Tell them: "Erase all 'I will be...' phrases that flash through your mind and onto your mental movie screens during meditation. Use the proverbial 'grain of mustard seed,' and say 'I am in perfect health,' 'I learn easily,' 'I understand everything I see, hear or experience and put it to good use'—or whatever else you want from life. No matter what your present situation, you should see only perfect results.

Say: "In meditation sessions, my young friends, you can turn 'maybe sometime' into 'I am now' through visualization.

When you see yourselves on your movie screen as having achieved your goals, your Subconscious Self will bring it to pass."

O Repeat the exercise until your students' Subconscious Selves get the message and start to change the situation for the better. You will know when that happens, for students who are training their Subconscious Selves will not want to continue once the Inner Self has ordered corrections.

O You can make this Building Block even more effective by playing baroque music (such as one of Mozart's works). Baroque music is a

powerful aid to learning. Set the volume of
the Mozart piece low, so your voice is easily
heard above the music. {I used baroque music
with astounding success to teach my English
101 college students how to write complete,
correct sentences.}

Say: "You are now in the healthiest possible
state of being. In this state you and you
alone will control your mind. No one but you
will ever control your mind. In this healthiest possible state of being, your mind is open
to learning. All that you hear, all that you
read, all that you see, you will understand
and be able to put to good use. The Light cre-
ated you so, and will help you learn with
ease, as well as solve whatever problems arise
during your life.

"You are beloved of the Light and of the
Universe. All you need to do is to close your
eyes, fill yourself with Light and pay attention to what you are seeing, hearing, reading,
or otherwise experiencing.

"You are a child of the Light and the
Light will help you gain the good that you
foresee on your mental movie screen.

"When you awake from this learning level of consciousness, you will understand everything you hear, read, see, or otherwise experience. To retain this clearness of mind, all you have to do is to remain calm, breathe slowly and fill yourself with the healing Light. Relax now, and know that even as your hear these words, the Light is busy making connections in your brain so you will continue to understand all you hear, read, see, or otherwise experience."

O While students are relaxing, present the new information you are teaching to your class. Present the new lesson slowly, in a soft voice, and explain as simply as possible.

O Choose material that some students have not mastered, and review it now—slowly, softly, simply.

O This technique is especially helpful in teaching multiplication and subtractions. Start with 1 x 1 and continue to difficult double digits to show students that repetition leads to over-learning—which eliminates counting on fingers.

Your lesson over, tell your students: "You are now in the healthiest possible state of being. When you bring yourself out of this state, you will be completely relaxed. Your Body will feel new-made and in perfect health. Your Mind will understand all you hear, read, see, or otherwise experience. Your Spirit will rejoice in the improvement of your Body and Mind. When you bring yourself out of this state of being, you will be filled with joy, a joy that will last for days."

O Conclude the session with **BLOCK XYZ.**

O Tell your meditators: "If your new-found mental ability starts to slip away, all you need to do is relax, breathe slowly and bring the Light into your head and body."

O If students have trouble with multiplications or fractions, tell them to repeat the difficult numbers over and over, for "over-learning" ends the problem.

O Tell the students that you would like them to write what they have learned about the Light, so they will have it for the future. Further, if they wish, their account will be placed in a class book so all may read about their work in the Light.

o Tell your meditation students they can summon the Light by just thinking about it, or by closing their eyes a second. Congratulate them on being so good and working so hard during meditation sessions.

o Add that you are setting aside time for more frequent meditations. Shorter periods and repetition, you can explain, should be more helpful than a single hour per session.

O Praise them, praise them, praise them for their hard work and cooperation.

o Praise yourself as well, for you have made it possible for them to start setting their family world—and your educational world— to rights.

o Update your log of meditation sessions and results, so you will have an accurate record of what occurred when and how.

O Identify information that students have had trouble understanding, and write your own Building Block to present to them.

O Everyone wants to do well, and you are making that possible for your students. Your dedication and hard work will earn you their lifelong praise.

## Prelude to Chapter 7

The following lessons will help students observe the obstreperous behavior of others—a non-threatening way of showing them what is required of a "child Of the Light."

Block L deals with rascality, and Block M with angelic influences. Examples can be the best way to preach.

# Chapter 7

O For additional meditations which can help your students, tell them to close their eyes and begin their Light work.

**BUILDING BLOCKS OF LIGHT**

O Begin as usual with **BLOCKS A to D.**

**BUILDING BLOCK L:** Request your students inhale/exhale the Light from above in order to build the Light within. When they feel relaxed, tell them that all of you are rising into the air and flying to a wonderful place. If anyone opens his eyes any time during meditation, tell him (as I did Lynn) that the Light within will leak out through his eyes and he'll become too heavy to fly anyplace. Treat it like a joke, of course. Children with disabilities are wary of criticism and you don't want to spoil the camaraderie you've built up during your sessions.

O Having reached your imaginary destination, a quiet house on the ocean shore, report how you feel about being there. Add a character to your story, as I did with the elf, and show him behaving in ways that are not acceptable. But associate the misbehavior with the character, and ask your group how they can help the other do right. Go easy here. Keep your character interesting to hold your group's attention, but complex enough so they don't discover the rascal's shortcomings are their own. Whatever else you do for your students, PRAISE THEM, PRAISE THEM for their interest and assistance. Let them know their good work for the character is appreciated.

O Ask your youngsters to invite the character to the seashore house you're "renting." An imaginary playmate in "your real home" might increase the character's disruptions, so you'll be keeping him on neutral ground. Ask your group to describe the outside of the house. How many stories does it have? How is it shaped? What are its colors? Have them walk the character to the door, knock, and be ushered into a living room. If, like Lynn, your students seem unable to describe the place, tell them to use the Light in their heads and they will see it.

O To avoid conflicting answers, ask them to focus on the misbehavior of their "guest."

Say, "Oh my, this guest of ours is being really bad. But maybe I'm wrong, so I'd like each of you, in turn, to tell me what YOU see him (or her) doing."

O When everyone is finished, ask what each of your students - in turn—think should be done about the guest's attitude. When the students finish, ask them what they can say or do to help the mischief-maker behave better. Listen carefully, for they may be describing personal experience, their own punishment and ways that might prevent their further misbehavior. Whatever they reveal, center attention on the "guest's errors" and praise them for helping the guest change his/her ways.

O Suggest that your students and the guest put on their bathing suits and rush out to the beach to splash around in the breaking ocean surf. Point out the warmth of the day, the delight in having a cottage where they can eat and sleep after they wear themselves out in play.

O Tell them: "This spot is yours—for as long as you want it. To return, all you have to do is close your eyes, fill yourself with Light and zoom in to enjoy the cottage and the ocean all over again. But right now, we need to go on to another Block of Light."

**BUILDING BLOCK M:** Ask students to visualize their guardian angel standing at their right shoulder. Have each meditator describe his/her angel and tell how he/she feels about being protected by this representative of Spirit.

Ask them to visualize the Light from above streaming into their heads and on down to the area of their disablement. If their problems stem from Sensory Integration Dysfunction, ADD, or some other neurological disorder which hampers their ability to learn, tell them the Light from above will act like a laser beam to "weld" the proper connections. (You may have to describe how doctors use laser beams to heal).

Tell them: "It's time to bring your mental movie screen in again. Put it in place and see yourself on your personal screen. See yourself understanding and responding correctly to all you see, hear, or otherwise pick up from your five senses.

Say: "Each of you is both director and actor of the scene being played on the screen. See yourself—not as you are now but how you would like to be, and engaging in as much joyful activity as you wish."

Add: "Now tell me, one by one, what is happening on your screen. If you're not the way you want to be, change it at once. Use your mind to put any inactive muscles of your body to work. If you are in a classroom, see yourself understanding everything and getting great report cards. See yourself jumping, running, laughing and having the best time of your life. See yourself doing all the good things that make you happy, and everyone else on your screen praising you for your success. Know that mind can work wonders with matter, and do not set limitations on yourself. Envision yourself as the great and good person you want to be and know that the Light will help you bring it to pass."

O If a student falls asleep during meditation, as Lynn and her father did during a June session, consider yourself fortunate.

Give him/her the most important instructions as he/she sleeps. DELETE NEGATIVE PHRASES from instructions. Instead of saying "You will not misbehave" or "You are being bad again," USE POSITIVE WORDS such as "You are behaving better" or "You are the best children I know. Thank you." Speak softly, confidently, as though what you want for them has ALREADY HAPPENED. Correct instructions describe the here and now, not the future. The sleeper may not be fully aware of your words, but during his nap his Subconscious Self will hear your message and begin to make desired improvements.

O Close the meditation with **BLOCK XYZ.**

O Repeat **Block M** during subsequent meditations until your students' Subconscious Selves get the message. You will know when that happens because they will be tired of the project.

O At that time only, start them visualizing their next "success" and wait patiently for the conditions they have "seen" on their mental screens to appear "in the flesh."

O Begin your regular teaching (to the syllabus) by asking everyone in the class to find his/her Light—even if it means teaching your entire class the pertinent Blocks of Light. Even great students have the right to know where the brain-power is most effective.

O With baroque music softly playing in the background, introduce new and possibly difficult information to your entire class for a preplanned 30-40 minute session. Speak slowly and just loud enough to be heard over the music. If students fall asleep, rejoice, for the information you are supplying will be even more deeply implanted than if they were awake.

# Prelude to Chapter 8

In a previous Block of Light, students observed the behavior of "others."

This time, Block N has them examining the effects of misbehavior on their own Body/Mind/Spirit.

Although the Blocks of Light have been arranged in alphabetical order, Counselors and Elementary School Teachers should repeat any Block for however long it is required.

It is advisable to teach all but the final Block at least once, but how you arrange the order or frequency will depend on your assessment of your students' needs and progress.

# Chapter 8

The light completes the first stage of
its work when it gives a child a sense of personal worth. But much remains to be done. People with mental, physical or emotional disabilities live in a restricted reality. Like
all of us, they create the sort of world they
think they deserve. If we or they dislike the
result, we can show them how build a better
one—using the Light within to alter the world
without.

Once children realize this is possible,
they are eager to get started. Lynn surely
was. And as she progressed, she became increasingly aware of matters of the Spirit. She
indicated this by describing the bridge on our
imaginary trip as purple—a heavenly color.

Even better, Lynn's exploration of her
Inner Self gave her the confidence she needed
to handle her ADD condition as well as Reading
and Mathematics Disabilities. These we dealt
with through meditation exercises and lessons
on the basics of both disciplines. Testing
followed the lessons, and were repeated over a

period of time to determine whether she was "developmentally" ready to retain information.

Children with ADD or similar learning problems may have faulty connections between brain cells and certain neurons. Given time, Light can and will forge links between brain and nerve endings. Retesting is needed to determine when the Light has finished healing.

One of our most powerful meditation tools is Visualization.

As was said before, WHAT YOU FORESEE IS WHAT YOU GET. If our lives are unsatisfactory, we can change them by Visualization.

Lynn Herson reversed her failures in Grades 1 and 2 by visualizing success in future school years. During an August 23 meditation, for instance, we explored every detail of an imaginary school day. Details of foreseen events provide a "reality" that carry over to "actual" experiences.

Olympic Game contenders have had great success with mental rehearsals. In "foreseeing" themselves turning in perfect performances, they build the mental and physical energies required to win medals.[8]

Focus on your students' "foreseeing" themselves under-standing all they see and hear. Show them also how to visualize them-selves behaving in ways that will keep them safe in all circumstances and all times. Repeat these meditation lessons until they put them into practice in daily life. That done, you are ready to introduce another Building Block which will teach them how to improve their behavior.

**BUILDING BLOCKS OF LIGHT**

Begin as usual with **Blocks A to D.**

**BUILDING BLOCK N:** Ask your meditators to imagine they are rising from their bodies to stand at their right shoulders with their own Guardian Angel. If necessary, explain that the mind can place its attention wherever it chooses. The choice this time is to be beside the Guardian Angel.

---

[8] Ostrander, Schroeder, Ostrander, <u>Superlearning</u>, pp. 151-193.

Say: "Now watch yourself sitting in a chair, your eyes tightly closed. But this time, instead of describing yourself, see yourself misbehaving. Whatever you do to get your way, see yourself doing it.

Add: "Now, with your Angel "standing at your right shoulder," I want each of you meditators, it turn, to describe how a parent or other adult is reacting to your demands." {Listen to each student, then say:} "Now imagine you're standing at <u>my</u> right shoulder, watching <u>yourself</u> whine and pester.

"Now, pretend YOU'RE the adult and I'M the whiner. The adult YOU is saying no to WHINY ME because what I want isn't right for me—at least now. How do you feel when I, that child, will not listen? How do you feel when I disturb the peace of our classroom or household? Is there a way you can end this disagreement of ours so we can be happier together?"

O Listen to their answers and plan for the next time they go "into their act."

Continue the meditation with, "You did that well, class.

Now everyone return to <u>your</u> right shoulder to stand beside your Guardian Angel. Look down at yourself. Then look inside your body and see what's going on in there.

"Very good! Now pretend someone is standing in front of you and is praising you. How do you feel about these compliments? How is your body reacting? It feels warm and comfortable and pleased, doesn't it?  Everybody's does. Approval makes us feel good all over.

"Uh oh. Here comes another person. He's a stranger and he looks mean. He is, too, for he's saying something nasty to you. And calling you names. Do the words or actions of this stranger make you "feel bad?" What's happening in your body, because of these "bad" feelings?

After all students reply, say, "It's best to ignore other people's opinions of us, for neither approval nor disapproval changes our inner self. So long as we are filled with the Light, we are perfect. Besides, the feeling and emotions which lead them to praise or blame us are their responsibility. If they say nice things, THEIR bodies will be comfortable. If they are mean and nasty, they poison their OWN bodies. Not ours. UNLESS we accept their opinions or actions. In that case, we give them the power to tell us how we should feel. What should we do, then?"

{Wait until all students respond, then add} "I think we agree. No matter how anyone treats us, that's THEIR PROBLEM. Our job is to fill them with Light. Though we may have to do this more than once, when they finally realize they can't "get to us and make us feel bad," they'll go look for other victims. That's be-cause we've killed their meanness with kind-ness.

Conclude your session with **BUILDING BLOCK XYZ**.

O Like Lynn, some students may doze off during meditations. If so, let them sleep. In relaxing, they slow their brain waves. On en-tering Alpha they begin to think and learn easily, but as they approach its lower level they begin to dream. A bit more relaxation and they can drop into the dreamless sleep of the Delta level. Each level is equally productive for implanting positive concepts.

{Lynn learned much about numbers during meditation naps. Light sleep eased her tensions and freed her brain to make nerve connections that often misfired in her waking state. But her improvement was temporary. Further meditations were required to help her brain make proper connections OR find alternate routes for understanding Mathematics.}

O Repeat meditations as often as required, changing the details enough to retain your group's interests.

O During your daily interactions with your class, look for changes in their behavior. Compliment them profusely on any improvements. Compliments will calm both of you. Criticisms and reprimands will throw both of you back into chaos.

O Concentrate, in meditation as well as daily life, on showing your meditation group Unconditional Love. Also, keep your own philosophies and beliefs to yourself so they can learn and grow in Divine Light.

O A few weeks of meditation should yield positive results.

Look for small gains at this point. The big ones will come later.

O Keep your log up to date, in order to assess your and your children's progress.

O Remember the rules for teaching meditation: UNCONDITIONAL LOVE and DETACHMENT.

O Remember also that in daily life you must be a firm and trustworthy educator. Your student does not need another playmate—just a reliable role model.

## Prelude to Chapter 9

Students who exhibit Behavioral Lapses after so many meditations may require you to assess possible reasons. As for results, Block O will show students that emotions are visitors which should be examined carefully.

Block P tells youngsters how to deal with bullies or other difficult people, and lets them practice handling a confrontation by visualizing a positive result.

# Chapter 9

Be patient if your students experience behavioral lapses, as Lynn did at the start of our September 7 meditation. Though it is deploring to hear falsetto "da-das" and perceive infant squirming in older children, behavioral lapses can occur. The uphill path to knowledge is rarely smooth. As Learning Curves show, steep rises in mental progress are often interrupted by brief dips or long, flat periods when the ability to learn seems to dry up. These dips and plateaus in the Learning Curve indicate students are assimilating knowledge gained in the previous rise. That done, their minds are clear for new advances.

If a child in your meditation group encounters one of these dips and reverts to earlier behavior, gently but firmly continue meditation exercises. When the session ends, analyze the regression.

I suspect Lynn's "setback" stemmed from excitement and the number of cookies she consumed at a gathering which preceded our meditation. Sugar—which becomes glucose in the brain—may affect ADD patients like her. Researchers at the National Institute for Mental Health found evidence to support the theory by using advanced brain imaging techniques to compare adult brain metabolisms.

The study documented that adults with ADD utilize glucose—the brain's main energy source—at a lesser rate than do adults without ADD. This reduced brain metabolism rate was most evident in the portion of the brain that is important for attention, hand-writing, motor control and inhibition of responses.[9]

But there is no single answer to ADD symptoms. Each patient is different. As a trained educator, you are in the best position to identify what distresses children. If you suspect certain foods or additives are affecting one of your students, suggest his/her parent consult a health-care professional about a change in diet.

Remind the parents that the human body requires things like minerals and trace elements to maintain its delicate balance. It needs salt, for instance, to build electrolytes

[9] A 1990 report by the New England Journal of Medicine on research conducted by the National Institute of Mental Health. Cited in Ch.A.D.D. Facts, 1995, Brochure 1, p.2.

to keep the body alive and well. Explain that they might risk their child's physical health by changing his/her diet on their own.

The child's emotional life, however, is in your capable hands, and you can continue to work on that with the following meditation.

**BUILDING BLOCKS OF LIGHT**

Begin as always with **BLOCKS A and B.**

**BUILDING BLOCK O:** Ask your students to look again within themselves and, one by one, tell you how they are "feeling" at the moment. Are they happy, sad, excited, bored, or what? Suggest they think about some joyful time and tell you when the joy "is over."

Suggest they recall a sad time and tell when the sadness passes.

Explain that: "Humans are neither 'joy' nor 'sadness.' These emotions come to us as visitors, stay a bit and leave. The fact that they are 'passing through' is a blessing, for it means we do not have to hang onto any 'bad' stuff. Anger, hate and the desire for revenge are just some of the 'bad' stuff we can do

121

without. They poison our bodies and keep us from growing 'healthy' in the Light.

Say: "Everyone imagine you are at your right shoulder and looking down at your body. Now recall a time when you have been less than an angel of Light. Perhaps you wanted to go somewhere and would not take no for an answer. Whatever the circumstance, right now look down and see what your irritation is doing to your body.

"Let's get rid of that irritation—or any other bad mood—by filling yourself with the Light. Ohh, it is wonderful that you have become a child of the Light. You are a joy to be with, and your classmates, as well as your parents, your friends and everyone else who knows you enjoy being with people—like you—who are filled with the Light.

Add: "Getting along with the rest of human kind is difficult for everybody, but especially youngsters. Building Block P may make it easier. This one teaches us how to deal with people who attempt to mistreat us. It may be someone who tries to build himself up by making others feel bad. Or it may be a neighborhood bully. Whichever, the Light will show us how to handle such people, without becoming upset, by using another Block of Light.

**BUILDING BLOCK P:** Say: "Do you remember the exercise where you stood at your right shoulder and looked down at your body? We're going to do something like that again. Only this time, the Light will help us deal with other people.

"First, find out who the bullies are in your school and keep out of their way. Report to school authorities if anyone threatens or tries to take advantage of you, and suggest that they put the bully in a meditation class so he can find his Light. But you won't need others' help if someone is saying mean things in order to hurt your feelings. The Light will show you how.

"Tell him, 'Gee, I'm sorry if you don't like me—or <u>anyone else. It</u> doesn't bother me, because I like you. I make it my business to like everyone. Being friendly makes me feel good. People who are angry or have other bad feelings poison their own bodies. Just stop a minute and tell me how you feel inside. Your body's hurting from being angry, and you're trying to get rid of your anger by hurting someone else. But that doesn't change anything. Your anger's still inside you, poisoning your body. Do you really want to do that to yourself?' Like most children, your students may need an example, so tell them: "Let's look at this another way. When you meet someone who tries to hurt you by word or deed, think of his ill will as a burning stick. If you take it and hang onto it, it will burn you. But that won't happen, will it? You're smart. You'll do what every smart person does—drop the burning stick and walk away. His or her opinion of you doesn't matter. Why do you care? You're filled with Light, and so long as you think and live in the Light, you have all the approval you need. Be polite to the person who tries to make you feel bad about yourself. Then surround her or him with the Light of Spirit and walk away.

"Let's practice that now. On your mental movie screen, see this mean person coming up to you and saying or doing something nasty. See yourself surrounded by the Light. Hear yourself telling him that in trying to hurt you, he is hurting his own body. Tell him you

like him and will continue to do so. See yourself surrounding him with Light and walking
away from him."

Conclude your double session with Building Block **XYZ**.

O Update your meditation log each session, recording all student actions, reactions, and any improvements in behavior.

O Check on the goals <u>you</u> set for your
youngsters, and note what else needs to be
done.

O Review the self-help schedules you and
your group agreed upon after the Building
Block **K** meditation in Chapter 7, assess their
progress and set new goals if needed.

O Honor their improvements by putting
their pictures up on your classroom bulletin
board and praising them lavishly for the Behavioral Adjustments they've made in a few
weeks.

O Be patient. With yourself as well as
them. You are giving your them the greatest
gift possible: a sense of being loved and
wanted by the Universe. And further blessings
will follow.

## Prelude to Chapter 10

Building Block Q is the answer to everyone's worst nightmares. It unmasks the hero of the nightmare (the dreamer) and shows him/her how to tame the beast.

Block R is another lesson on using the Light to overcome bad habits and thus purify one's emotions and body.

# Chapter 10

At some point in meditation teaching,
children might tell you they REALLY DO NOT see
the Light when they close their eyes. Other
people may have convinced them no Light exists. Or their doubts may have sprung from
personal experience. It makes no difference.
Explain calmly and gently that it is not un-
usual for distorted faces or weird landscapes
to drift across the closed eyes of people who
are falling asleep. Scientific investigators
have named these visions Hypnagogic and Hyp-
nopompic Images. Many people see them. Perhaps
your students will not, but the fact that they
are visible is important. Tell your students
that we need Light in order to see pictures,
whether our eyes are open or shut. Further,
they need not be alarmed if images appear. If
they are annoying, meditators need only tell
the images to leave them alone in the Light.

Next, ask your students if they ever had
a good dream or a nightmare. It is a reasonable query. Everyone dreams and children are
apt to remember. If anyone replies "night-

mare," tell them you will talk about that in a minute. Right now, you need to know whether their dreams include people. Also, do they dream in black and white or in color?

The questions are red herrings—ones that lead up to our explanation that everybody needs Light in order to see people, whether in monochrome or color. But one cannot see anything in the dark, so all who envision people in dreams are Lighted within, even in sleep.

Say: "This inner Light does not blaze like the sun. Oh no, it shines soft as a fingernail moon. It brightens, however, each time we work with It, and if we continue long enough, our closed eyelids may become bright as a full moon."

Children love scary stories and thrill to the excitement of scary costumes at Halloween, but put the same story or costume in a dream and they will scream down the night. But who can blame them? Bad dreams are no respecters of age. They terrify adults, as well as youngsters—UNTIL we learn how to deal with them.

Dream experts tell us that nightmares are the outgrowth of tension and stress in waking life, but that people can prevent them. Adults

benefit from being taught how, but youngsters
have a desperate need for such knowledge.

## BUILDING BLOCKS OF LIGHT

O Tell your students: "This Building
Block will tame your nightmares. We get bad
dreams because we're afraid of something or
fear we're failing, somehow, in daily life.
When that happens, our Unconscious Self brings
the fear to our attention so we can deal with
it. And we shall."

O Begin your session with the basic
Building Blocks of Light, **A to D,** then say:

**BUILDING BLOCK Q:** "Let's talk about nightmares, shall we? Nightmares—isn't that an odd
name for a bad dream? You know where it came
from? Across the ocean. From England, the
country that started the English language. Now
once upon a night time, hundreds of years ago,
English people were afraid to go out in the
dark. Electric lights hadn't been invented
yet, so unless the moon was at least half size
and no clouds dimmed its light, it was dark
indeed. Good folk, as they called themselves,
went to bed with the sun. They feared the

night, believing that one of the evils that
lurked outside their homes was the spirit of a
female horse—a Mare. It ran wild, they told
each other, searching for people it could
trample to death. That's why the good folk
called it a Nightmare. Well, that was super-
stition. We know there's no ghost horse gal-
loping through the night—or the day. All we
have left of the fearsome horse is the word
for bad dreams—NIGHTMARES. And we're going to
rid ourselves of them now.

"First of all, the Light protects you.
Waking or sleeping, your inner Light can keep
you from harm. When you dream, certain problems or fears of daily life can appear as monsters. You need not be afraid of them. The
Light has made you a hero—that is, a person
who can overcome all problems. The Light gives
you courage to rid yourself of any monsters
who show up. All you do is face them, zap them
with Light and they'll turn into something
small or friendly. Or they'll disappear in a
puff of smoke. Don't be afraid to face them.
The Light protects you from harm. Now, pretend
you're dreaming that something's chasing you.
You run fast, but it follows. You hear it com-

ing up behind you and feel its breath on your back.

"Stop running, everyone. Good. Now! Turn around and zap it with Light. There. See that? The frightening creature became a warm puppy. Or a friend. Or it went "poof," leaving nothing to see or fear. You're the hero of your dream. The Light is pleased with you. So am I.

"This week, every night before you go to sleep, practice turning around and facing a monster. Then, if you dream of one, you'll remember how to put it in its place. I'm going to do the same, in case I have a nightmare."

O Facing a nightmarish creature requires great courage. If your students fail at first, do not give up. Repeat the Building Block that stresses the power of Light to help them overcome fearsome sleep experiences, as well as those of waking. In so doing, you will be the teaching hero of an heroic child.

O Follow up on this serious matter with a Light exercise that can be sheer deLIGHT:

**BUILDING BLOCK R:** Say to your students: "Now let's explore another helpful Building Block. You have already learned two ways of entering

Light. The first is by finding it. The second is to breathe in and out slowly. We'll now combine these methods to increase our use of Light.

"With your eyes still closed, see the white Light that shines down on you from above. It surrounds you, forming an egg shape with you in the middle. This Light extends about a foot from the widest parts of your body and on every side, including above and below.

"Do you see it? Good. You'll use your breath this time to push that Light out from your body. I'll do it, too, and count for all of us. We'll take a deep breath and as we exhale, we're going to bring the white Light all around us, including above our heads and below our feet. You ready?

"Wonderful. Take a deep breath and hold it a second. Perfect. Exhale and watch the Light expand to two feet in every direction from your body. Ohh, you did that well.

"Breathe in again. Hold it. Now breathe out and expand the Light to three feet in every direction. Hold it a second.

"Breathe in and hold your breath. Breathe out and push the white Light to four feet. Hold it a second.

"Breathe in and hold your breath. Breathe out and push your Light to five feet above, below, and all around you. Breathe in and hold.

"Exhale and expand the white Light to six feet. Look how big it's become. Inhale and hold your breath.

"Exhale and expand the white Light to seven feet from every part of your body. Breathe easy now.

"Oh, how well you did that. Your Light and mine have joined and are shining so white and bright. But we don't want to leave it that way, so we're going to bring it back close to our bodies.

This time we'll inhale and shrink the white Light a foot each time. As we exhale, our Light will throw off any dark colors it may have picked us from us being unhappy. We have to throw off the bad stuff because we need room to pack the white Light around us. You all set? Then let's go.

"Inhale and bring the white Light in to
six feet in every direction.  Exhale and throw
off all the bad stuff. You're doing fine, students.

"Inhale and bring the white Light to five
feet.  Exhale and throw off all unhappy junk.
Wonderful.

"Inhale and bring the white Light to four
feet.  Exhale and throw off any aches, pains
or worries you might have. Ah, fine.

"Inhale and draw the white Light to three
feet.  Exhale and clear out any anger you
might have about anything. Great.  Exhale and
get rid of any leftover bad stuff.

"Inhale and shrink the white Light to two
feet in every direction, including above your
head and below your feet.  Exhale and expel
any bad feelings.

"Now, one last time. Inhale the Light to
one foot from the widest parts of your body.
Exhale and see the pure white Light pack itself around you. Once again each of you is
standing in a brilliant egg shape of Light.

"With your eyes still closed, look down
and see the Light below your feet seal itself

off. Look up and watch the white Light above your head seal itself off.

"We enjoy pushing out our Light to several feet in every direction because it makes us feel good. And if we're ill, we can throw off whatever is making us feel bad by expanding the Light and then bringing it back to one foot from our bodies. There just isn't room for aches and pains in close-packed white Light.

"Usually we leave the top of our Light Body open so we can get more Light from the Spirit, but there are times when it's best to seal it off. If someone threatens us or makes us feel even a little uncomfortable, we should seal our Light off at the top. It is packed hard around us then—too hard for other people to get through.

"This egg shape of Light is called an aura. Keep it close around you, students. It will protect you day and night. If you think any bad stuff has found its way into your white Light, open it up a bit when you're alone and clean it out again.

"Know that as long as you keep your aura rainbow-bright, it will help you to do what is right every minute. And let me tell you a secret. All colors combine to make white. White Light is perfect and it expects you to act perfect—that is to be kind and gentle with others who may not have as much white Light as you."

End your meditation with **BUILDING BLOCK XYZ.**

O I taught Lynn how to use her aura when she played a role in Nutcracker Suite. Star performers "shine better" than less noticed actors, singers or musicians because, prior to taking the stage, they gather their forces. Actors say this period of silence is to put themselves "in character." Actually the experts are building energies (the Light) that they send out to their audiences. The result is called "Stage Presence."

O It worked for Lynn and will for everyone, once they become comfortable with the technique.

## Prelude to Chapter 11

Everyone on earth gets what he/she thinks he/she deserves. This being so, discontent with the status quo merely requires one to program the Body/Mind/Spirit for better results. (Former college students who wanted a particular automobile with a specific color programmed for their desires and reported they got results within two years. Several adult meditators claim they were encouraged to start new careers and have succeeded beyond belief. The author of this work located a beautiful farmhouse and farm whose two-hundred and fifty acres were being advertised for about a million dollars. Though able to afford less than $100,000., she claimed the house and sixty acres for her own and within three months her family moved in. What you foresee is truly what you get).

Block S tells your students how to visualize what they need or want on a movie or TV screen, and so train their Subconscious selves to produce results.

*Margaret Laurie*

Slow learners or misbehaving students often lack good friends. Block T will show them how to get them.

# Chapter 11

By this time you should be seeing improvements in students' behavior and learning ability. Though they may still appear minor, they should be plentiful. The Light builds self-respect, and inner progress promotes outward improvement. Health care professionals call this Behavior Modification. As improvements surface, congratulate your students for working so hard. And yourself, of course, for finding ways to better their lives.

You have taught your neediest youngsters how to slow their brain-waves from the Beta Level, where humans juggle input from the five senses, down to Alpha. Minds are calmer at that stage of consciousness, so your students can think and problem solve much more effectively. Thus, if they act up, calmly and quietly suggest they take a "time out" to find their Light.

Do not expect a steady upward progression in their behavior.

Their symptoms may recur often until they learn to control them. Be patient. Understand that lapses in behavior are not their fault and will yield to proper encouragement. Their improvements since you started the meditation sessions testify to the importance of your work with them.

Your personal training of your students is the best and quickest way to Behavior Modification.

## BUILDING BLOCKS OF LIGHT

The next meditation is designed to show the existence of Light within and reinforce the benefits to be gained by fore-seeing. Move cautiously on the foreseeing, however. Your students will all profit from learning how to use the Light to get what they want and need. But first they must improve their mental and physical selves. They will discover soon enough how to use the Light to accumulate material things. Let that be later when they, and not their parents, are paying the bills.

## BUILDING BLOCKS OF LIGHT

o To prepare for this meditation, visualize a clothing shop that carries garments of reasonable cost, and in sizes and styles appropriate for your students. The Block of Light is designed to show the existence of the Light within, and to reinforce the benefits to be gained by foreseeing.

Begin the lesson, of course, with **BUILD-ING BLOCKS A-D.**


**BUILDING BLOCK S:** Say: "Close your eyes, please, and bring out your mental TV screen so we can go to the mall. You've outgrown some of your clothing. Let's go into this shop and look for new ones. They have racks of garments for both boys and girls to choose from, so each of you find your size. Also, your favorite styles.

"Ahhh, here's your favorite color. Or would you like another shade this time? But remember. Even in a well lit shop like this, colors look different under fluorescent lights than they do in natural daylight.

(Pause a moment) "Come to think of it, you're seeing this on your own mental movie screen. Your eyes are shut, yet you saw the shop, racks of clothing, and all colors of the fabrics, didn't you? That's because you have Light within you.

The Light is also there when you dream. It has to be. No one can see dream people and things in the dark, can they?

"Oh look, there's a dressing room. If you find something you like, try it on. It fits perfectly, doesn't it? Look in the mirror and you'll see. Do you like that color? The style? Look at the price tag, too. Is it something your parents can afford to buy you—especially when you grow out of all your clothes so fast?

"If so, remember what it's like so you can find it when you REALLY go to the mall. Don't worry. If you truly want it, it'll be there. What we foresee is what we get."

{Speed up the process by keeping the girls in one shopping area and the boys in theirs, but give each student a chance to choose a garment and discuss it with you).

O {You may even wish to take all of your students to two shops—one for boys who might prefer clothes from a sports emporium and another for girls who prefer department stores. But wherever your imaginary shopping spree takes you, foresee what their families can afford—at least until your meditators master the art of foreseeing themselves in possession of ample funds.]

O If, despite your precautions, a student wants to purchase something costly, faddish or otherwise inappropriate for his or her age, discuss the matter after the close of meditation. Explain that you and everyone else wants them to have the best things in life, but they might have to wait until they grow up and earn them on their own. Remind them that things of the Light are more lasting and precious than worldly goods.

O Explain as well that while clothes are important to keep the body warm or cold, they should not be an indicator of a person's worth. The inner self is what matters, not the outward trappings.

O Tell them: "Ah, I bet you're thinking that if you don't have the right clothes, you won't have any friends? But you'll be wrong, because right now we're going to use the Light to help you attract and keep suitable playmates."

O Tell them that to get friends they must be one. Explain that they will need to like people and be considerate of them. Ask them to

start looking at other children, find ones
they admire and make a list of their good
qualities. Discuss each possible friend—
omitting names, of course—with the rest of the
meditators. Spend time on this, for you are
teaching them how to choose good friends. Hun-
ger for playmates can lead to poor choices.
Tell your students that as "children of the
Light" they will want to associate with children who live up to its principles.

Help your students ignore differences in
financial status or social position, as well
as race or creed. They need to establish
healthy relationships, ones that will help
them survive the turmoil of adolescence. Help
them choose friends who value affinity of
Spirit rather than the trappings of a materi-
alistic world.

O When students find someone whose likes
and dislikes coincide with their own, suggest
they learn what interests that potential
friend. Be it dinosaurs or Barbie dolls, ad-
vise your meditator to learn about the subject
so he and his potential friend will have something to talk about.

O Tailor your instructions to fit the age group and specific interests of your students. Having done all that, shift your focus to meditation **BUILDING BLOCKS T.**

**BUILDING BLOCK T:** Tell your group: "Our next important business today is to discuss looking for and making good friends. That's not easy for anyone, my dears, even grownups like me. But there are some things we can do to help ourselves.

"First off, we have to keep ourselves under control. Everybody jumps around once in a while, but who wants to put up with constant commotion? Or with people who change their minds every few seconds? Not the sort of friends you're hoping for. They'll expect you to keep yourself and your emotions in check.

"Next thing is to study people and find ones you admire. That can be tricky. People act different ways at different times. If you like someone because he (or she, if that's the case) is smart in the classroom, you may disapprove of the way he acts at lunch. There, he might hang out with a little group and refuse to talk to you or other 'outsiders.' Before you judge, though, try to figure out why he behaves that way. Is he shy? Is he more comfortable with a small group rather than a crowd? Or does he sit with boys who like the same things he does?

"Ah, there's a clue, honey. Find out what he likes. Pay attention to what he says. Notice what he reads. Look at his clothes. Are they trendy or just average? Does he wear jewelry?

If so, what kind? Is he good in gym? In music? Art? Whatever he does, praise him when you see him. Don't make a big deal of it, though. Also, don't stare at him. You don't want to give the impression you're prying into his business.

"Let him know by compliments and smiles that you think he's wonderful. Everyone wants to be liked and he'll give you credit for recognizing his worth. But all the time you're admiring who he is and what he does, get ready to talk to him about one of his favorite subjects. That means you'll have to spot what it is and learn something about it.

"During all this, forget about yourself and what YOU want.

It's all right, dear. You have the Light. You know it makes you special, so you don't need compliments. What you do need is friends, and the way to make them is to be kind and considerate to everyone. Show interest in people of all ages. If they turn out to be dull, remain friendly but start looking for more exciting people.

"The word will soon get around and you'll have more friends than time to spend with them.

"Once you become popular, you'll need different rules. Observe them carefully. Don't let anyone in your group draw you into disliking or feuding with someone else. Youngsters do that often. Jim can be best friends with Doug on Monday, and hate him the rest of the week. If you side with either Jim or Doug, you may lost both as friends when they make up. Never take sides.

Find everyone worth your loyalty and then "Speak as you Find" and with love in your heart for all. The Light expects Its children to love everyone.

"Also, let others in your group choose an activity or even lead the crowd, if they want to. If they plan something that could harm themselves or others, suggest a suitable alternative. Don't do anything wrong, no matter what. You have to answer to a higher judge, the Light."

Conclude the session with **BLOCK XYZ.**

O Repeat the guidelines for making friends until your students become some of the most popular people in school. And they will be, if they stick to the rules.

O Though you may not believe popularity is important, consider your students. Some, if not all, have learning disabilities that have kept them outside the candy store. Now you're showing them the way to OWN the store. Don't begrudge them the chance to be a part of society—particularly during their coming teens.

If your students become peer-oriented, don't fret. That's apt to be a temporary phase. Because you taught them to meditate, they will develop the habit of liking others and, sooner or later, go on to more serious work in the Light.

## Prelude to Chapter 12

Building Block U is a light-hearted adventure—a suitable reward for students who have attained full control of self and improved their ability to learn.

Building Block V is preceded by information about auras and continues with a lesson in finding the Light which surrounds every living thing, whether fauna or flora. Seeing auras is a valuable tool for Counselors and Teachers—inasmuch as they will be able to spot and avert trouble in the making. And those troubles will lessen when students realize they can't hide wrong intentions.

# Chapter 12

We have nearly completed the set of twenty-four Building Blocks. During the weeks you taught your students Blocks A through S or T, their learning and behavior skills should have improved. But each child is different, and it may be that some of them require more time. Be assured, however, that continued meditation will lead to improved behavior and ability to learn. Maintain a positive attitude. It will happen.

When your group is comfortable with Blocks A through T, they will be ready for a new challenge. Continue their meditation sessions as long as they benefit them, of course, but at this time begin to stress the importance of their putting these meditation lessons to work in daily life. Meditation is their interior work. Transferring those interior gains to the exterior world is YOUR job, and it is a vital one for children with all sorts of learning or behavioral disorders.

Best of all, it is easy. Your worst experiences with this group of unruly students is behind you. Now you must help them "fine tune" themselves for progress.

This readiness requires we change the Building Block format.

Though Blocks **U, V** and **W** will be offered in the usual way, meditation sessions will now emphasize "exterior" gains. It is important for your students to put what they have learned to proper use in daily living. In so doing they will prepare themselves for their crowning accomplishments, full control of THEMSELVES PLUS THE ABILITY TO LEARN.

You will be given step by step instructions for guiding them to self control shortly. Right now, let them enjoy another imaginary journey.

**BUILDING BLOCKS OF LIGHT**

**BUILDING BLOCK U:**

After introducing introductory Blocks A to D, tell your students:

"Today we are going to take a special trip, so fill yourself to the brim with Light. Is everyone ready? Then fasten your seat belts. It's lift-off time and we're going up,

up through the ceiling, through the roof of
our building and into the air.

   "It's a dull day, isn't it? But that's
the way we want it. We're heading for the
clouds and will look for a special one. Most
of those I see are too white and fluffy.
They'll do for transportation, though, so
let's hop onto one. Wow. I got a soft seat.
How about you? Now, students, I want you to
take turns steering this fluff of air around
the sky until we find a cloud chock full of
rain. You can do it. Your mind is in control
and whatever you imagine you can bring to
pass. Pretend there's a steering wheel stick-
ing up in front of you. Grab hold of the wheel
and head toward the horizon.

   "Keep your eyes on where you're going,
though. I'll look for our rain-cloud. Humph.
Slow down a bit until I find a landmark to
tell us where we are. Oh, oh. I think that's
the ocean down ahead of us. Better turn
around. We want to land on ground, not water.
Ahhh, that was a smooth turn. You're doing
fine. We're heading back toward home base now.
Hey, look. There's a possible rain-cloud on
our right. Slow down to cruise speed and move

up over it, so we can see if it's the one we want.

"Ahh, do you see that? It's full of rain, sure enough, but its drops are too small. If we went down to earth with that cloud, we'd have to grab several raindrops in each hand to use as parachutes. Let's look for something better. Hey, steer toward that dark cloud on our left. Whoa now. Move above and around it, so we can see what it's made of.

"Yep! That cloud's perfect. Its raindrops look like sparkling colored beans in a jar—the kind that jump around. But each raindrop is as big as a basketball. Let go the wheel and everyone take my hand so we can drop from this fluffy white cloud into the dark one. Ready? Here goes.

"Choose one of the big raindrops and let your feet sink into it. Good. I'm standing in the one in the middle of all of you. Oh look, the water's running up over our legs and hips. Now it's covering our chests and necks and heads. Well, what do you know? Each of us is in a separate bubble, and its rainbow colors are swirling around and into us—making us calm and happy. How peaceful my bubble is. And how

beautiful. Tell me, class, what colors do you
see in your rain bubble?

O Give each a chance to identify the colors.

O Choose a park in your vicinity and ask
your students to look down at it and tell you
what they see. If they do not mention picnickers and youngsters playing on swings or
slides, ask them to find some below so you can
come down nearby.

"We're sinking fast. Take my hand so we
won't be separated.

Whoosh. We're so heavy we made a hole in
the bottom of our cloud. An enormous hole. The
other big drops are pushing us down. Guess
we're the first drops of the rainstorm. Hang
on. We've going in for a landing. (Give a pretend moan) You know what? We're raining on
family picnics. People see us coming down in
our great blobs of rain. What do you think
they'll do?

{Wait for their replies.}

"Get ready. We're landing. When we reach
ground, our bubbles will burst and water the
grass. Look. People are sitting under shelters
or in their cars so they won't get wet. Steady

now. Bend your knees so you'll land comfortably. And, if you like, pick a spot next to a picnic table, where we can sit and rest up from our trip down to the park. Oh look! The picnickers are watching us. Do you suppose we're sitting in their places?

O Ask your students to describe some of the picnickers, then continue.

"They'll come back soon, I imagine. The rain's over. We made such a big hole that our cloud dumped all its rain at once.

We'll leave before the people return. They might want to know where we came from, all of a sudden, and why we didn't run for shelter when the sudden shower began. We could tell them, though I doubt anyone would believe we came down from the clouds.

O Add your own details and ask questions that will stimulate the children's sense of participation.

Then say: "People are coming back, so let's go. Filled with Light as we are, we'll zoom up into the air and head for home."

But don't leave now. We have another VERY important Building Block, V, that you won't want to miss."

O Your next lesson deals with the bodies of Light that surround living things. A review of the history of the aura in Western Civilization will prepare you to teach your youngster about it. BUILDING BLOCK V will phrase this information in words more suitable to children.

Tell them: "During the Middle Ages and early Renaissance in Europe, artists often painted auras (halos of light) around the heads of holy subjects. During the next few hundred years, "rational people" rejected the idea of light bodies or "auras." Attitudes began to change, however, in the Twentieth Century."

{The following is basic information which you will probably wish to explain in simpler terms:

{About 1911 a book called **The Human Atmosphere, Dr.** Walter Kilner reported the first "scientific sightings." As physician and surgeon of a London hospital, Dr. Kilner invented the Kilner Screen to view his patients' auras.[10] Unfortunately, his findings did not impress his medical peers.

{The next notable "sightings" were made by a Russian couple, Semyon and Valentina Kirlian, whose high-frequency photography captured the light bodies of plants and humans on film. Publication of Kirlian books during the 1960s prompted five scientists at the Kazahk State University in the Soviet City of Alma-Ata to publish a paper on the Kirlian effect in 1968. These five people claimed that all living things have a physical body and a "double"—a separate entity that emits an electromagnetic field. Instead of referring to it as an aura or a "double," the scientific group called it a "bioplasmic body." The energies of both physical and bioplasmic bodies, they added, are built and maintained by breath. They also said that people with low bioplasmic energy are prone to disease.

{Kirlian photography intrigued Viktor Adamenko, a biophysicist who lived next door to the Kirlians. In 1972, Adamenko reported

[10] For further information, see: W. J. Kilner, The Aura. New York: Samuel Weiser, Inc., 1974l; Sheila Ostrander and Lynn Schroeder, Psychic Discoveries Behind The Iron Curtain. New York: Bantam Books, 1874; Edgar D. Mitchell, Psychic Exploration. New York: G. P. Putnam's Sons, 1974.

the existence of human energy fields in four papers for the <u>Journal of Paraphysics</u> and presented another paper at the Moscow Parapsychology Conference. Western scientists began to take note.}

{The aura—or whatever else anyone wishes to call it—was no longer just a symbol used by Medieval and Renaissance painters of holy people. Modern individuals might not understand it, but many decided it must exist. Reputable experimenters had said so.}

O Knowing there is scientific evidence of the Light will help you teach Building Block V. Begin by explaining the previous information in terms your students will understand before you offer this "waking" exercise.

O By now you and your students should be familiar enough with relaxation techniques to use them with open eyes. If you wish to see auras, you and they must be completely at ease.

O For this new "seeing," find a room that has just enough light to see the outlines of your hands. Besides dimness, you will also need an empty wall. A plain surface is necessary, so if the room is papered, suspend a sheet from the ceiling or drape it over a curtain rod.

O Position yourselves about a foot from the plain surface.

O Since this exercise requires open eyes, do not begin with Blocks A-D. Simply ask your students to stand (or sit) with you in the dimly lit room.

**BUILDING BLOCK V:** Say: "Listen, everyone. Do you know some people can see the Light that surrounds humans, animals, and other living things like bushes and trees? They call what they see an Aura. When we go to the library I'll show you pictures of paintings and stained-glass windows where figures have circles of light around their heads. The artists used these halos or auras to show that the people in their paintings were holy.

"That's the usual explanation, anyway. Now we suspect some artists may have seen the Light around good people and decided to add IT to figures representing God and Angels.

"Not everyone believes in auras, though. Lots of people say there's no such thing. But those who SEE the Light that surrounds people

and things know auras exist. Would you like to
see your own aura? I would. We'll have to relax, though. Let's pretend we're so relaxed
that our bodies are stuffed with rags instead
of bone and muscle. You ready? Good.

"Now hold your hands above your head as
you face the plain surface. Open your eyes
wide and stare at the top edges of your fin-
gernails. Easy does it. Stay relaxed and
practice staring. You'll know when you do it
right because your eyes won't blink. Take your
time, dear. Keep looking at the tips of your
fingers.

When you keep your eyes open wide and un-
blinking long enough, you'll see a faint glow
around your fingers. It may appear darker than
the wall behind it or lighter, like cellophane
or plastic wrap.

"Go easy. If you become the least bit excited when you see it, it will disappear. If
that happens, blow out your breath and relax
again. Stare at your fingertips again. Do that
as many times as you need in order to extend
your aura seeing."

O When you are certain all have seen the
faint aura, ask two of your students to stand

before a mirror—saying all of them will have the chance.

Tell them, "Look into the mirror and focus on the top of your head. Relax every part of your body. Breathing slow will help you relax, so take a couple slow breaths. Good. Now widen your eyes and stare into the mirror. Pick a spot about an inch above your head and focus on it. If you're blinking or your eyeballs move, you won't see the aura. Your eyes have to be wide open and staring at that spot above your reflection in the mirror. I'm looking at your reflection, too, and I'll tell you when I see your aura.

"Just remember, auras disappear if we get excited when we see them. This is lazy work, so be calm. And keep looking."

o Continue the exercise until all your students have had a chance to see their 'bodies of Light.'

O Aura sighting is important for two reasons. First, your students' faith in the Light—as well as yours—will be strengthened by "seeing" it surround their bodies. Second, knowing it is there will help learning dis-

abled children to put the Light to use in everyday life.

Say to them: "You have used the Light
within and around you to help you learn in
school and to calm you when you become over-
excited. The Light's shown you how to control
your body. But that's been inside work. Now we
must use the Light for outside work: around
the house, in school, and every other place we
find ourselves.

O Repeat the exercise any time it is con-
venient. Do not wait for meditation sessions,
for BLOCK V is meant to build a BRIDGE of
Light from the inner Self to "the real world."

O And when that happens, you'll know that
the Body, Mind, and Spirit of the Self is
working in the Light.

## Prelude to Chapter 13

Building Block of Light W is the final and one of the most needed Blocks for children (or grownups) who have suffered physical or mental abuse.

I pray you will not need it, but will teach it to the best of your ability if required.

Thank you for leading children—and possibly grown-ups, out of heart-breaking troubles into the Light of the Universe.

# Chapter 13

The remaining Building Block of our set
is not necessary, I hope, for children with
ADD or other learning disabilities. Until after I finished my work with Lynn, whose problems did not include those addressed in Block
**W**, it never occurred to me to consider the
subject. And I pray you can ignore it, for
youngsters with learning problems have enough
to overcome without adding abuse to the list.

Nonetheless, Block **W** is a fitting conclu-
sion for our set of meditations. Abused youngsters need help from the Light more than anyone in our world.

The reasoning behind Block **W** is best
stated in **Dr.** Carl G. Jung's observation in a
German publication. The noted psychiatrist and
Depth Psychologist said:

> I have often seen individuals simply
> outgrow a problem which destroyed others.
> This 'outgrowing'...was seen to consist
> in a new level of consciousness. Some
> higher or wider interest arose on the
> person's horizon, and through this widen-

ing of his view the insoluble problem lost its urgency. It was not solved logically...but faded out when confronted with a new and stronger life-tendency. It was not repressed and made unconscious, but merely appeared in a different light, and so did indeed become different.

What, on a lower level, had led to the wildest conflicts and to panicky outbursts of emotion, viewed from the higher level of the personality, now seemed like a storm in the valley seen from a high mountaintop. This does not mean that the thunderstorm is robbed of its reality, but instead of being in it, one is now above it.

Our goal, therefore, is to show the abused youngster how to rise above the traumas inflicted on him in his "helpless" years.[11]

O Plan carefully before you begin work with a youngster who has been wronged by assault from an adult. Abused children are apt

---

[11] Richard Wilhelm, The Secret of the Golden Flower; a Chinese Book of Life. Foreward and Commentary by C. G. Jung. English translation, Cary F. Baynes. New York, 1962.

to distrust all grownups. You will need to earn their trust. To do that, it would be best to find a meditation partner of the opposite sex to assist you in talking about the Light.

Naturally, an abuser should NEVER be allowed to teach any of the Building Blocks, and Block **W** in particular. This especially applies to any parent who has victimized his youngster. Children cannot trust their abuser, even if the latter has reformed, and without trust in the teacher, the Building Block program will fail.

Fortunately, teaching meditation to children is a job well suited to educators or responsible parents. Abusers are rarely adult enough to read about the subject.

But anyone who teaches meditation must carefully lay the groundwork for Block W. Victims must know that their parents and other adults blame the abuser, not them. Discuss the matter with the child beforehand, and continue through the meditation to assure him or her that he/she is innocent of wrongdoing.

Your teaching team for Block **W** may include a parent, but stop at two adults. The presence of more could overwhelm a child who is already heavily burdened.

If the parent is not the team partner, proceed with care. You do not wish to expose an abused child to another predator. Fortunately, you will find dozens of individuals who are decent and caring and willing to heal the injured soul. Someone who has been teaching meditation to his or her own child is a possible team-teaching partner. A member of the clergy, a doctor or trained counselor who will agree to assist a "non-professional" is another option.

A team of both sexes can help ease the victim's fear of the sex that caused the trauma. Continue Team-Teaching for as long as it takes. When you are certain the child feels safe and comfortable in your presence, you may dispense with assistance and teach your child on a one-to-one basis.

However you begin, give the youngster a teddy bear or some other stuffed toy to cuddle while you deal with his/her terrible experiences.

O Begin in the usual way, with Blocks **A** to **D** and tell the child that after you work with the Light you will take him/her on a mar-velous trip. But first, the student must fill self and Teddy with Light so they will be "light enough" to fly away.

## BUILDING BLOCKS OF LIGHT

**BUILDING BLOCK W:** Replacing the boy's or girl's name with HONEY, say: "Listen, HONEY, we're going to talk about your importance to the universe. The Light within you wants you to know It loves you, and you are precious to It. That may seem hard to believe, considering what you have been through, but it is so.

"You are special, Honey—so special that the Light wants you to be happy. Up to now, you haven't been. That's not your fault. The person who hurt you is to blame. He (she) never found his own Light. And he's weak. He may seem strong to you, because you're little and he's big. But he's weak, so weak that he needs power. So weak he's unable to deal with people his own size. He has to hurt children like you to get power. He's sick.

He picks on people who can't fight back. You know that. Worst of all, he's made you feel dirty, guilty and worthless."

O If the child has been a victim of sexual abuse, continue with Option 1. If he or she has been beaten or mentally abused, skip to Option 2.

**Option 1:** Say: "The Light wants you to know you are not to blame for what that terrible person did to you. You had no choice. But you do now. If he (she) or anyone else ever tries to force you into doing what you know is wrong—the Light will show you the difference between right and wrong—tell your teacher, school counselor, or the head of your church. Or the police. In our country we have laws to protect children from attackers. Report what has happened. Don't let the shame you may feel hold you back. You have nothing to be ashamed of. Your abuser is the only one to blame, and sooner or later will have to pay for trying to destroy you. Your abuser is sick, in head as well as heart. He (she) never found the Light within. All who have the Light protect children rather than do evil things to them. And make no mistake. You may not be the first

child he (she) has treated like garbage. Or
the last. These sick people go on and on, until children they harm become old enough to
tell them to stop, or get help to make them
stop.

"I'm proud of you, Honey, for getting
through such terrible times. When that adult
was hurting you, you could have imagined you
were somewhere else. Or someone else. Whatever
you did, you detached from yourself, Honey.
Many of us do when we're helpless. Good thing,
too, for how else could we make it through
such terrible times? Now you're going to imagine something wonderful, the Light inside
yourself. The Divine Power of the Universe put
this spark—we often call it the "spark of
life"—within your chest when you were born. It
is the Light of perfect good, a healing Light
that will help you love yourself. It will
teach you how to be happy about who you are
and where you're going. It will also help you
understand where you've been.

"This tiny Light within your chest was
put there by the Power of the Universe. At
first we pretend we're going down into our
chests and examining every part of it until we

locate that pinpoint of Light. When we find it and build it into a bright Light, we will know it's not our imagination. It's real. As you'll discover for yourself. When you find the Light and work with it, you will be happy with who you are, with where you're going in life, and will understand where you've been.

O To continue sexual abuse lessons, skip the following paragraphs and resume with #.

**Option 2:** If the problem stems from another type of physical or mental abuse, say: "The Light wants you to know you are not responsible for that adult hurting you. That person did such a terrible thing to you because he (she)cannot handle life and takes out his (her) anger on those who can't fight back. People like that have never found the Light in themselves. If they had, they would have protected you instead of doing such awful things. Men and women who don't have the Light and who take advantage of children are not fit to associate with a fine child like you. That awful person made you feel bad about yourself, but Divine Light will make you feel worthy of Its presence. You are a child of Divine Light and are loved by God and the universe.

"If this person tries again to hurt you or someone else in your family, get away quick. Report him (her) to the police. Even if he (she) is your parent. Being a parent means more than just bringing a child into the world. It means loving and caring for children, not hurting them.

"The Light wants you to be happy and you cannot do that if you live in fear. If your other parent cannot protect you from your abuser, ask the police or someone in your church of school to move you to a safe place. Better to be away from people who hurt you and make you feel unworthy of being loved."

# For all types of abuse, continue with:

"You are a child of Divine Light. As such you are a beloved of God and the Universe. This is a blessing you will repay by living a good and decent life.

"Dear child of the Light, wherever you go or whatever you do, Divine Light will love and comfort you if you fill yourself with It. In searching for this tiny spark, you are looking for what people call 'your own SPACE.' When you find it, the Light will fill that space to the brim, for it is the Light of goodness. The

Light will flush out the bad feelings you got from being abused. Not all at once, of course. You will have to work with the Light and it will take time for you to realize you are pure and innocent—inside and out. But it will happen. The Light loves you and wants you to live as a good and decent person. It wants you to become a Light-giver, because no matter what you do or where you go in life, you take yourself. Let that self be a Child of the Light, one who knows that the Light has flushed out all the bad stuff that has happened. You may never forget what happened, but you will not carry the bad stuff around with you. This is important, for when you get older and go out into the world on your own, you need to feel you are worth as much as the best people. Which you are. You have been wronged. But you've DONE NO WRONG and are as good as the best on earth. Maybe better, because you have overcome terrible times and are living as the Light wants—doing only good things and knowing you are worthy of good in life and death.

"Can we practice working with the Light now, Honey? While you have us two adults to help? Let's begin, then. Take a deep breath and bring the Light from above down through the top of your head and into your chest, where it will join the spark of life within you and build a powerful Light. Let your breath out.

As you do, you will throw off all the body pain and sadness this bad person caused you.

"Now you know how to do it, let's breathe in the Light and breathe out all the bad stuff. For seven times. I'll count and breathe with you. Ready?

O In a soft, gentle voice, pace his (her) breathing slowly for seven inhalations/ exhalations.

"Thank you, Honey. You did that perfectly. I'm proud of you. So is the Light. It sought you out, Honey, because you've been a good and brave person. The Light wants you to be happy. It will help you be, if you let It. Here's what you have to do: when you start to think no one cares about you—close your eyes and find the Light within your chest. Build that Light with the help of Divine Light that God pours down on your head. God loves you and wants you to know you have been chosen to work in the Light for your own good and the good of the world.

"God's Light will calm and protect you. It will teach you how to guard against people who do bad things to others. It will show you how to live in harmony with good people—who far outnumber bad ones. It will remain with you by day and night and will enable you, when the time comes, to join your Light with that of the Divine Power. Our Light and what we do with it during life are the only things we take with us when we die. By doing good to people and other living things, we take only good with us, in both this world and the afterlife.

"One more thing. If you have bad dreams or flashbacks about your terrible experiences, quickly build your Light and It will banish them. What you've been through is past and done with. The Light will guide you to a good life, if you let it. And I know you will, for you are brave and strong. I'm proud to know you.

"Now, you've earned a treat, so we're going on an imaginary trip. It will be fun, for when you put your mind to use, you can go whenever and wherever you please."

Repeat **Block W** at every meditation. Abuse causes horrendous damage to the human psyche. A child's body can heal fast. His Mind and Spirit may take years to recover, even with meditation. In being denied true love and at- tention, victims have difficulty building a healthy self-esteem. They are apt to be plagued by feelings of worthlessness and de- spair. In finding Divine Light they will find themselves, for they will learn that they are special to the Highest Good in the universe.

O When teaching **Block W,** take the child on an imaginary journey—one from the **Building Blocks** or one of your own design—to show he (she) is worthy of enjoyment.

O Conclude the session with **Building Block XYZ.**

O Children who have been abused, as well as children with learning disabilities, need to feel they are an important part of the uni- verse. Through no fault of their own, they have been exposed to stressful conditions. Thus, once you have eased the trauma of abuse with **Building Block W**, bless the child further by teaching him/her the entire set of Blocks.

O Helping another human being find he/she is valued by the Universe is the greatest gift you can give to mankind, as well as to your Self.

**THE END**

*Margaret Laurie*

# About the Author

My children were infants when I came down with a non-transmittable disease that several doctors said I would have for the rest of my life. In healing this disease, I started my journey into the Mind, Body and Spirit of the Self. Years later, my interest in Mind/Body/Spirit revived when I discovered many of my college students did not know how to learn. Research uncovered information about brain levels, and within a few months I had written a college course that included literature as well as brain-training. My colleagues approved a trial run of 15 weeks for 3 hours of college credit. My first students—ranging from new High School graduates to educators with Ph.D.'s—were so enthusiastic that my Division allowed me to continue teaching "Insight to Learning" for 15 years. The Mind/Body/Spirit book, <u>Centering Your Guide to Inner Growth,</u> was published in 1978 and is now in print in five languages.

In the late 1990's, a former meditation student insisted I teach meditation to her eight year old grandchild, who had ADHD.

Building Blocks of Light resulted from an hour a week teaching this youngster how to learn. The book begins with two chapters about her experiences, and moves on to the Building Blocks which will help other children master their disabilities.

To help college students learn "how to learn," Professor Margaret Laurie devised and taught an accredited course in Meditation for fifteen years at Niagara County Community College. Her meditation book, first published in 1978, is now printed in five languages.

In the late 1990's, a former meditation student asked Margaret to teach meditation to her eight year old grandchild, who had ADHD. A year of one hour a week sessions turned the child into a calm, competent and confident student. These sessions, repeated in *Building Blocks of Light*, will enable Elementary School counselors and teachers to work similar miracles in their classrooms.

Printed in the United States
23223LVS00001B/180